I WAS NUMBER 87

I WAS NUMBER 87

A Deaf Woman's Ordeal of
Misdiagnosis, Institutionalization,
and Abuse

ANNE M. BOLANDER AND
ADAIR N. RENNING

Gallaudet University Press
Washington, D.C.

Gallaudet University Press
Washington, D.C. 20002

Library of Congress Cataloging-in-Publication Data

Bolander, Anne M.
    I was number 87 : one woman's story of misdiagnosis,
institutionalization, and abuse / Anne M. Bolander and
Adair N. Renning.
        p.   cm.
    ISBN 1-56368-092-0
    1. Bolander, Anne M.   2. Deaf women—United States—Biog-
raphy.   3. Deaf children—United States—Biography.   4. Deaf
children—Abuse of—United States.   5. Deaf children—Education—United States.   6. Deaf—United States—Biography.
7. Diagnostic errors—United States—Case Studies.   I. Title:
I was number eighty seven.   II. Renning, Adair N.

HV2534.B63 A3 2000
362.4'2'092—dc21
[B]
                                                    00-028788

⊚ The paper used in this publication meets the minimum re-
quirements of American National Standard for Information Sci-
ences—Permanence of Paper for Printed Library Materials, ANSI
Z39.48-1984.

Stoutamyre, the school I describe in this book, was in full operation for the five years I spent there. When I went back twenty years later, the only things still standing were the building we lived in and the gym. When they go, the only thing left will be the memories.

I sincerely hope that this book will help other children with as-yet-undiagnosed hearing problems to be spared the horrors that I experienced.

Anne M. Bolander

PREFACE

I don't believe in coincidences. I think we are where we are supposed to be, and we meet people along the way who help us to get there. I am convinced that the purpose of my entering a multilevel marketing company—something I'd never in my wildest dreams thought about doing—was to meet Anne Bolander. (I was a miserable failure at multilevel marketing, so I know the purpose wasn't to be successful in that field.)

My sponsor in the company, knowing that I had written and published a book of my own, told me of a friend of hers who had an incredible story to tell and asked if I would perhaps be willing to offer her some suggestions on how to get it published. I'd had so much help with my own book—help that I could never repay except by passing it on—that I agreed to meet with her.

Our mutual friend had already told me some of Anne's story before I met her. My first impression of Anne was that she was a very bright but shy and self-effacing woman. I was amazed at the accuracy with which she could speechread.

Over the years Anne had asked several friends to help her organize her manuscript into a book. Some had even taken it home, only to return it untouched, sometimes as much as a year later. So she was understandably reluctant to turn the large, white, loose-leaf binder containing her life story over to a total stranger. After several meetings over Slim Jim sandwiches at Big Boy's, we agreed that I would take the manuscript home and let her know within two weeks if I wanted to work on it.

As I read Anne's neat, precise script, I knew this was a story that needed to be told. But it would need a lot of work. Because Anne thinks in American Sign Language, the work needed to be "translated" into grammatically correct English. Also, there were gaps that needed filling and events that needed elaboration.

Early on, I realized that some of the information in the manuscript would require verification. Anne was born with a severe hearing loss, but was misdiagnosed as retarded at one of the country's most prestigious hospitals. She was then sent to a privately-owned school for retarded children. Anne's description of her early life was the stuff of made-for-TV movies, and the school's director made Nurse Ratched in *One Flew over the Cuckoo's Nest* seem like Mary Poppins. Clearly, before this book could be published we would need to establish that others could validate Anne's memories. I acquired a telephone book from Bridgewater, Virginia and began making calls and placing ads in the local papers.

It wasn't difficult to find locals who remembered the Stoutamyre School for Special Education, and after only a few days' research I had accumulated a notebook full of others' recollections of years of abuse, both physical and emotional, inflicted on the already challenged children placed in the school's care. While initially none of the people I spoke with remembered Anne by name, the stories they told paralleled Anne's memories.

As we worked, I shared what I learned with Anne, and in some cases the information served to unleash a flood of repressed memories. For example, Anne had originally chosen to use a pseudonym for her book, and had selected the name "Debbie Bailey" without knowing why. Even though in Anne's memory, all the children went by numbers, somewhere in her mind was the name Debbie Bailey. Debbie Bailey, I found out, was a real person, one of the students at Stoutamyre School, and I was able to talk to her sister. While at my house on Easter Sunday 1998, Anne had a breakthrough and suddenly remembered Debbie Bailey clearly. Debbie was Anne's secret friend. Sadly, Debbie died more than twenty years ago, so a reunion was not possible.

In the effort to provide as accurate a record as possible of Anne's life, I questioned her relentlessly for a year and a half. However, she simply cannot remember some things. Some events are too painful, others lost in her prelanguage years. But to the best of our ability we have recreated Anne's story . . . a story of misdiagnoses, neglect, and abuse, but also a story of hope.

PROLOGUE

I have no memory of my birth mother. Others have provided all the information I have about her. Once, while rummaging in my grandmother's dresser, I found a picture of a young woman who looked a lot like me. I held the faded black and white picture next to my face as I looked in the mirror and could easily see the resemblance. I looked more like her than like my father, Warren, or Pat, the woman I had thought was my real mother. *Who was this woman? Why had I never met her? And who was the woman I had thought was my mother for sixteen years—the woman who persuaded my father to send me away?*

My earliest memory is of living with my grandparents. My twin brother, Peter, lived there too for a while, until one day our father came and took Peter home with him. I was about three years old and didn't realize I was just too much of a handful for my parents.

For a while, both of my grandparents worked—my grandfather as a butcher and my grandmother as a telephone operator—but eventually my grandmother stopped working so she could spend more time with me. She took me to a nursery school for a few hours every morning. I was a handful there too. I wouldn't sit still during story time because I couldn't follow what was said. I was bored, hyperactive, and threw a lot of tantrums.

I stayed with my grandparents until I was nearly five years old. Then, in the spring of 1959, my grandparents gave up and my father came to get me. Warren and Pat took me to their home in Virginia. Besides Peter, there were three other boys living in the house!

Warren was hardly ever home, and Pat had her hands full. I didn't listen to her any more than I had listened to my grandparents. I had been living with my family for about a year when I walked into my bedroom to find a suitcase lying on my bed, filled with my clothes.

Pat and Warren seemed very happy as we left on our "little vacation." It was late summer, a beautiful sunny day, and I was dressed in shorts and a T-shirt. I was one month shy of six, and I remember the ride clearly because I had never been in the car for so long before. The scenery changed as we left the familiar buildings of the city. We passed through farmland and pastures filled with animals—sheep, cattle, and horses. Then we were on an expressway. *How can this road be so long with no traffic lights?* I wondered.

We left the expressway and again entered farming country. From my perspective in the backseat, trees and telephone poles whizzed past. Finally my father turned off the main road onto a smaller narrow one that led to a huge brick building. A very large woman came through the doorway to greet us. Pat gave her a hug and told me her name was Margie. We sat outside while Pat and Margie talked. I had no idea what they were saying: that Pat and Warren were leaving me there and my life would change forever. So I lay on my back in the cool grass, counting the big fluffy clouds overhead.

Margie held my hand tightly as Pat and Warren got into their car to leave. I tried to run after them, sure that they had forgotten me, but Margie kept holding onto my hand and wouldn't let me go. As Pat and Warren were waving good-bye, Margie took my arm and made it wave back. I was confused; this wasn't my grandmother's house. They left me there, my suitcase next to me, in a strange building. My grandparents were not there. My brothers were not there. Who were these people? Still gripping my hand, Margie led me inside. The car was still moving away down the long driveway. I watched out the window as it got smaller and smaller until I couldn't see it anymore. I sat down beside my suitcase to wait for them to come back. I waited for a long, long time, but Pat and Warren didn't turn around to get me. I was six years old, alone and terrified, and no one knew that I was deaf.

The large woman who held my hand as my parents drove away turned out to be Margie Stoutamyre, the owner of the Stoutamyre School for Special Education. She and her two sisters had bought some property near Bridgewater, Virginia, and had adapted a large building to house fifteen boys and fifteen girls. Some of the children were mentally retarded, some had physical deformities. They came from all over the United States and ranged in age from six to eighteen years.

Margie was responsible for the children and had several supervisors to help her. There was also a maid and a man who came to do repairs and mow the lawn. He was there so often that for a long time I thought he was related to the sisters. One of Margie's sisters, Stella, was in charge of the office. In the spring she planted flowers in the gardens and window boxes. The other sister, Florence, also lived there. She and Stella had bedrooms in the front of the building, but we rarely saw either of them.

~The two-story brick building where I sat waiting for Warren and Pat was on twenty-five acres surrounded by pastures and farmland. The location was very quiet and many miles away from everyone and everything. There were no gasoline stations, stores, or banks. There were no children riding bikes, no dogs, and no ice cream trucks.

The building was like a huge box and had fancy white trim on the roof and lots of six-foot-tall windows. The side entrance led directly to the dining room. The room's long wooden table was pushed up against the wall, and had thirty wooden high-backed chairs facing the wall.

Two cooks prepared the food. They would be gone for a short while and then they would be back again for a long stretch of time. Years later, I figured out that the cooks worked during the week and had the weekends off. When the cooks weren't there, the rest of the hired help was also not there. Otherwise, all the days were the same.

A door opened from the dining room onto a hallway that led first to the stairs going to the second floor and then to the front of the building. The first landing up the stairs led to another stairway that led to the playground. Further up the stairs were two dormitory-style rooms, boys on the left, girls on the right. Margie's room was between the two bedrooms. Both bedrooms were about 800 square feet and had eight sets of steel-framed bunk beds with steel springs and thin plastic mattresses. Everyone was allowed one pillow and one blanket with their sheets. There was a bathroom for each bedroom, with a shower area and a smaller room with one sink and one toilet.

Downstairs, the reception area and Margie's office were right next to the dining room. Margie's office had a desk, a file cabinet, and a few couches. A hidden doorway led to an eight-by-ten-foot room that was completely empty—no furniture, no mirrors, no electrical outlets, nothing. This was the punishment room, but not the only one. In one corner of the dining room was a trap door leading to the root cellar where all the produce was kept. Sometimes children were put down there, too, in the damp darkness.

Outside, the playground was divided in half. On the boys' half were swing sets, a baseball diamond, and a basketball court. Boys occasionally threw a ball around but I never knew if they were playing a game or not. The girls' side of the playground had swing sets and long benches under an ancient oak tree. Between the two playgrounds were picnic tables and an enormous brick barbecue pit where the groundskeeper cooked hamburgers and hot dogs for everyone on warm summer weekends.

Another large building was used as a gymnasium in the winter and on hot summer days. The gym was also divided into two halves by a line on the floor. Everyone knew that line was not to be stepped on or crossed over. It was one of those things we all learned the hard way.

Margie had two supervisors on duty in the daytime and one in the evening. In the five years I was there, I never knew any of their names. A maid was there every weekday, cleaning and mopping the bedrooms and bathrooms. She also filled the little cup of baking soda that we used to brush our teeth. The cooks were in charge of the dining room and the kitchen. They prepared the food, washed the dishes, cleaned the table and the thirty chairs, and mopped the floor.

No one's name was ever used; I didn't know what a name was or that I had one. We all had a number. I was Number 87. (After leaving Stoutamyre, I learned to count and recognized the symbol that had been my number. Perhaps I was the eighty-seventh child to live there.)

Every day was the same as the day before and the day after. To wake us in the morning, the cooks rang the dinner bell, a huge thing which was mounted on a wood post outside the dining room. The bell was so loud that even I could hear it. If a child didn't get up immediately, the supervisor on duty rang a smaller bell in her ear until she did. We stood at the foot of the bed with our bunk partner, waiting. Bathroom roll call didn't start until we all were out of bed.

My turn in the bathroom came after the girl called Number 86 was finished using the toilet, washing her face, and brushing her teeth with the baking soda. (I got so used to the taste that I had trouble using toothpaste when I went home for visits.)

We had to wait at the foot of our bed until everyone was done before we could begin getting dressed. Our uniform was a maroon and black plaid jumper with a white blouse, white bobby socks, and penny loafers. The boys wore black slacks and white shirts. All of our clothes were numbered, even our underwear and shoes. When everyone was dressed, we marched single file down the stairs to line up behind our chairs in the dining room, waiting for the signal to sit down.

After we were seated, the back legs of our chairs had to be on the solid black line on the floor behind us or we wouldn't get a meal. We all sat facing the wall. After the supervisor checked to make sure all the chairs were lined up, Margie brought each of us a pill. Each child had a different color pill; mine was white. Margie would watch to make sure we all swallowed our pills as we waited to be served. I didn't know the name of my pill, just that it didn't taste very good without water and that after taking it my reflexes were slow.

When everyone had been served, the supervisor on duty gave the signal to begin. (Even though I never heard a signal, there must have been one because everyone else began eating at exactly the same time.) Then, and only then, were we allowed to touch our silverware. We unfolded our napkins and put them in our laps. We had to keep our backs straight, our heads up, and our eyes looking straight ahead at the wall in front of us. We were to raise our forks to our mouths, and if anyone's head dipped to take a bite, a hand came from behind to shove the guilty child's face into his or her plate. If anyone accidentally spilled milk, he or she waited for a supervisor and then licked the milk off the table. Nothing was wasted. We had to eat everything we were served, even if it meant sitting at the table for hours.

4

Breakfast was usually oatmeal and toast or pancakes and sausage. On weekends we had cold cereal and toast. Hot meals were served in the middle of the day, and usually soup and sandwiches were served in the evening. For the noon meal, we had meat with a vegetable or two and applesauce. Everything that was served had to be eaten but we couldn't have seconds. Creamed chipped beef on toast was frequently served, as was liver and onions. Jell-O was the most common dessert. The vegetables all came in cans and the meat was frozen. Milk was delivered twice a week in huge stainless steel jugs that were hooked by plastic tubing to the milk-dispensing machine.

When everyone was finished, we were given the signal to put our silverware on our plates. Each piece of silverware had its place—the knife at the top of the plate, sharp edge toward us; then the fork, perfectly lined up next to the knife; then the spoon—and any student who didn't put the silverware in the right place couldn't leave the table. Lastly, our napkins were refolded and put in their original spot. When we stood, we pushed our chair under the table and waited for the signal to turn right. Then we marched outside, single file, while the kitchen staff started to clean the dining room.

The daytime supervisors came to the playground to watch us while Margie ran errands or did her paperwork. Margie and each of the supervisors carried a belt or a whip at all times, and they always found reasons to use it. (Even I could hear the crack of the whip when one of the children misbehaved.) However, we didn't have many rules on the playground. As long as we stayed within the boundary lines, we could do pretty much what we wanted. We could swing or just sit under the old oak tree, but we couldn't touch each other. No physical contact or communication between the children was allowed. Everyone wandered around, minding their own business, in their own little world; the little pills we were given had done their job.

This was the time we could move our heads when we wanted to, rub our eyes, scratch that itch on our nose, or even pick our noses if we felt the need. Yes, there were other children on the playground, but I blocked them out of my vision for my own protection. Because any type of interaction between children brought punishment, I stayed in my own world.

I usually took this time to feel my arms, my legs, my head. I tried to capture the feeling of what it would be like to touch another human being. *Would it feel the same way if I put my hand on their hand? Did their bruises hurt like mine did? What would it feel like to run my fingers through another person's hair?* My fear of punishment was too great to risk trying to find out. I learned to appreciate the warmth of the summer sun and the wind in my hair, and the clouds constantly shaping and reshaping themselves as they floated overhead. I was sad on completely clear, sunny days because there were no clouds to tell me stories.

While sitting on the lawn I watched the insects going about the business of survival—bees flying from flower to flower, ants carrying crumbs to their holes in the ground, the mosquito burying its long nose in my arm. I followed them, fascinated by their busyness and purpose. I loved watching a bird fly to the ground and grab a worm, then fly off to its nest in the tree above me. Once I came upon a caterpillar transforming itself into a shining chrysalis. Although I didn't know what it was called, I watched as it hung upside down, enveloping its body in the shimmering silken threads. Daily I returned to the ancient oak to make sure it was still there. And in the spring I watched in fascination as the chrysalis split open and a butterfly climbed out. I held my breath as it unfolded its beautiful wet wings and stretched them to dry in the sun. Then it flew away. I was both sad and exhilarated; if it could change and fly away, maybe I too could leave someday.

Exploring our surroundings was never boring because our perception of the world was so limited. Going outside was a time of peace away from the cruel people who ran Stoutamyre—a vacation from the prison-like existence on the inside.

At lunchtime the bell rang again and everyone lined up to march inside.

The lunch and dinner routine was the same as breakfast. Sometimes after supper in the summertime we were allowed to go back outside again, but usually we were marched back upstairs to the dormitories. We once again stood in pairs by the foot of our bunk to wait for our number to be called for our turn in the bathroom. When everyone was finished, we changed into our nightclothes to watch television (one channel only, and if the set had volume, it was never loud enough for me to hear).

We had shower night once a week—one night for girls, the next for the boys. On shower night, instead of putting on our pajamas after dinner, we stood naked by our bunks until all were ready. Then we marched, all fifteen of us, into the shower area. Margie was at one side of the doorway with the soap and shampoo. The water was already running as we walked in, one at a time, to get wet. We then returned to Margie with our hands cupped to receive the liquid Ivory dish soap. We had no washcloths. After we lathered our bodies and rinsed off, we returned to Margie again, this time for a small amount of shampoo for our short hair. After each girl was finished, she went into the next room to dry off and wait until Margie ordered her to stand at the foot of her bunk. When everyone was showered and dressed in pajamas, we had bathroom time before bedtime. Anyone moving too slowly heard the crack and felt the sting of Margie's whip on her skin.

We didn't have much to do at Stoutamyre. We were always glad when the groundskeeper cooked hot dogs in the barbecue pit, because the dining room rules didn't apply when we ate at the picnic tables. In the winter, if it wasn't too cold, we could play outside in the snow, though we weren't allowed to throw snowballs. When the weather was bad, we went to the gym to play catch, always with the supervisor watching us to be sure the boys didn't play on the girls' side or vice versa. The supervisor's whip quickly found anyone who crossed over the line, even by accident. And, of course, no talking or laughing was allowed on the playground or in the gym.

I knew of no classrooms. When we were not eating, sleeping, on the playground, or being punished, we sat around doing nothing. The only way to avoid punishment was to obey the rules exactly, and in time we came to seem like robots. Looking back, I think criminals in prisons are treated better than we were. At least they can read, study, attend church, and go to the bathroom when they want to.

We had no toys of any kind. The only things I could call my own were my clothes, my comb and brush, and my toothbrush. Once a girl's parents gave us each a stuffed animal. As long as her parents were there we were allowed to hold the little stuffed bears, but as soon as they left, Margie came around and took the teddy bears away.

We never celebrated birthdays or holidays. I didn't know what a birthday party was. And Margie didn't like to let us go home because it took too long for us to adjust back to the routine when we returned. Sometimes we were allowed to go home for Christmas holidays, if our parents could come get us.

Although there weren't as many rules at home, life with Pat and Warren had one thing in common with Stoutamyre: punishment. Pat thought Margie could do no wrong and firmly believed that whipping was the best way to control the behavior of her young, retarded daughter. Maybe she thought that other people wouldn't understand her philosophy, because she always made sure nobody except Warren ever saw her punish me. Years later, when I told her about the o[ther] terrible things that happened to students at Stoutamyre, [she] didn't believe me. The only thing she believed was that I had been whipped—which was, to her, a normal punishment for someone like me.

I didn't understand that there were two worlds—one at Stoutamyre and another one anywhere else. Even a few days away made our return really hard on Margie. The number of punishments always increased after visits home.

Like Numbers 1 through 86—all the children before me at Stoutamyre—I learned the hard way what to do or not to do to avoid being punished. Our main goal every day was to keep the supervisors and Margie happy. The newcomers always had it worse because they didn't know the rules. It was easy to tell how long a person had been there by the frequency and severity of their punishments. As I got closer to the end of my stay I was punished somewhat less often.

My first punishment was a spanking while I leaned over a chair with my hands and feet on the floor. After a time, many of the spankings blended together until I couldn't remember what that first one was for. Although she sometimes used a board with holes in it, Margie's favorite tool was a belt and she always had one with her. When one belt wore out, she got a new one, which was always very stiff until it was broken in. The other supervisors had Margie's permission to punish us for any infraction, but Margie was the master when it came to punishing children.

Margie's sisters, the maid, and the cooks weren't allowed to have any contact with us. When we were punished, they acted as if nothing was going on. They were pretty good at turning their heads to avoid seeing what they didn't want to see. They knew they would lose their jobs if Margie saw any sign of disapproval in their faces. Once, one of the cooks was caught helping us cut our food; we never saw her again. Even the adults at Stoutamyre had to follow the rules.

The typical punishments—slaps or spankings, with or without a belt—were carried out in full view of whoever was around in the dining room or on the playground. Even though we weren't supposed to watch, we couldn't help knowing what was going on. The worst punishments were carried out in private.

A child who was about to break a rule was never warned. No one said, "No, don't do that," or "Put that down or you'll get it!" We learned after the act that it was against the rules. I quickly learned that if I laughed, cried, or tried to make sounds, I would get smacked. On the playground, away from the supervisors, I tried to form words and mimic how they talked. I was fascinated with the sounds people made, even though I couldn't understand anything they said unless they yelled and were facing me. One day, while in the dining room, I forgot and almost said a word. Margie heard me and stalked over to the table. I stiffened to take the blow as she raised her hand. She hit me across the face so hard that my eye swelled shut and my lips went numb. There were no mirrors at Stoutamyre and I wasn't allowed to touch my face, so I didn't know how bad it was until I was under the covers that night.

The hardest thing for me to learn was not to scratch my head in the dining room. An accidental scratch brought a very deliberate blow that left my head spinning. I soon learned to hold my head very still following the blow to keep from getting hit again. The rules in the dining room were very strictly and swiftly enforced. Every day someone got spanked or had their face shoved in their food.

Almost as bad as disrupting the dining room routine was interfering with the daily bathroom roll call. We were only allowed to go three times a day: before breakfast, after lunch, and before bedtime. If someone had the flu and had to go at another time of the day, they were spanked. If they didn't make it and had an accident in their pants, they had to clean themselves up and then they were spanked twice—once for making a mess and once for not following the bathroom rules.

The Stoutamyre School wasn't much on academic education, but it did provide endurance training. One punishment for the younger children was kneeling for hours on the hard floor. Another supervisor might make a girl stand with her back against the doorjamb and her feet about twelve inches out at the bottom. Then she had to squat down and stand up, over and over until her legs gave out. If the punishment for a boy was push-ups, only his nose could touch the floor. If anything else touched the floor, he was whipped with a belt.

I received my worst punishment when I was ten years old, after I had been at Stoutamyre for about four years. My grandmother had taken me to the 1964 New York World's Fair. We ate at restaurants, she bought me gifts, and, best of all, she hugged me. I was so starved for affection and simple human contact that when she brought me back to Stoutamyre, my heart broke. I wanted to run after her car and go home with her.

That night, after all the lights were out and the room was quiet, I caught myself crying. Terrified but unable to stop sobbing, I covered my face with my thin pillow, knowing that soon the lights would come on and Margie would be standing over me with the belt.

I pictured myself running away from Stoutamyre. I envisioned my grandmother welcoming me into her home to live with her. Excited by my plan and with my mind filled with images of my grandmother, I managed to stop crying and climb out of my bottom bunk. I snuck out the door, past Margie's bedroom, and down the hallway to the stairs.

Outside! I was free! I ran down the half-mile-long driveway to the road. I don't know how long I walked down the dark country road. We had no concept of time at Stoutamyre, just the cycles of eating and sleeping, dark and light, cooks and no cooks.

Margie had known when I left, but she didn't stop me. She wasn't worried. After all, how far could I get? And where would I go but to the road? Our world ended at the end of the driveway. She waited a while, then sent the maintenance man in a car to pick me up.

Walking through the door, I could see her standing in the hallway smiling at me. It was a chilling, evil smile that meant I was going to be spanked. *Okay,* I thought. *I'll get spanked and tomorrow it will all be over.* I couldn't have been more wrong.

Margie had a table in her office with straps in each corner. She had me take off all my clothes and lie face down on the table while she buckled the straps around my wrists and ankles. She picked up her belt and started to whip me. Usually a few hard swipes with the belt was enough, but this time the beating went on and on until I couldn't stop screaming. The more I screamed, the more she whipped me. Finally she stopped and unbuckled the straps. No sooner had I sat up carefully on the table and pulled on my pajamas, when Margie grabbed me by the arm and pulled me up the stairs to her sleeping area. She pushed me into a chair, then used a rope to tie my legs to the chair legs and another rope to tie my hands behind my back. She put a broom up the middle of the chair back to keep me sitting straight. I spent the rest of that night tied to the chair.

The next day Margie put the other supervisors in charge of the rest of the children so she could devote all her time to me.

She waited until the others had left for breakfast before untying me and taking me back down to the table. I didn't see anyone on the way. Once again I took off my pajamas before she strapped me down and began beating me again. When she was done, she took me upstairs where she tied me to the chair again and left. Later she returned and untied me long enough to go to the bathroom before she went to lunch. I was exhausted, hungry, and in terrible pain. The maid, whose name I never knew, came to wipe the tears from my eyes and went to Margie's snack stash to get me something to eat. No doubt she was listening for Margie's footsteps on the stairs as she quickly brought me water and then went back to work as though nothing had happened.

I endured two more days of whippings, being tied to the chair, no sleep, and no food before Margie felt she had taught me a sufficient lesson. After the last beating I collapsed to the floor in a bloody heap when I tried to walk. Margie kicked me to make me get up, but I couldn't move. She threw me into a small room with no lights or furniture. When some of my strength returned, I crawled away from the door but lay so I could see light coming through the crack under the door. I waited to feel vibrations on the floor: Margie's footsteps. When I had to go to the bathroom, I went to another corner of the room and then went back to my original corner to lay down.

I had not eaten for so long that I was past being hungry. My mouth was dry and my tongue felt like toast. My muscles were in knots, and I was afraid that if I fell asleep Margie would wake me up and beat me again. I went to my bathroom corner when I had to, and after awhile the room began to smell pretty bad.

I don't know how much time had passed when Margie finally opened the door. It was daytime, and the sunlight nearly blinded me as Margie dragged me up the stairs and put me in my bed. Nice, soft bed, at last.

As she left, Margie gave the maid something to put on my sores. The maid gently took off my pajama bottoms, and with a washcloth and warm water, she tried to wash away the blood. I screamed when she touched my legs with the salve. She brought me food when she was finished, but I couldn't eat. Later, when the others came in from outside and saw me, they couldn't react or even look in my direction or it would be their turn for a beating.

Punishment at Stoutamyre was something we never, ever forgot.

2

Rather than an occasion for mercy and kindness, any kind of sickness was just another punishable offense. Every year or so a doctor and nurse would come to give each of us a physical exam. They would look in our eyes and ears, put a stick in our mouths, and tell us to say, "Ah-h-h," while they shined a light down our throats. They would listen to our chests and then give us a lollipop when the exam was over. But only occasionally was a nurse called for children with colds or the flu, or even the mumps; usually we were sent to bed and Margie took care of us.

The flu made its rounds through Stoutamyre like at any school, but the consequences were different for us. One day we came in from the playground and sat down for dinner, and I knew something was wrong with the boy next to me because he couldn't sit still. While the rest of us were eating, he was holding his stomach and moving around in his chair. I had just taken a bite when he vomited all over his plate and part of mine.

I turned to look at him—it was a reflex—and saw the supervisor coming toward us. I thought she was going to punish the boy for vomiting, but instead I got slapped for turning my head. Then she noticed the vomit on our plates. Had I not turned my head I might have gotten a fresh plate of food, but my punishment for looking was to finish eating what was on my plate, vomit and all. Everyone else was finished and had gone to the bedrooms before the boy and I were done. I finished before the boy did and was taken upstairs by another supervisor. Now *I* was feeling sick to my stomach. I spent my time in the bathroom vomiting up what I had eaten. We were limited to only a few minutes in the bathroom, so I quickly wiped the toilet clean and went to bed.

During the night I threw up all over the pillow and under the covers. I knew I would get spanked if Margie found out, so I pushed all the vomit under my pillow, but I couldn't hide the smell.

Morning came and we were all supposed to be standing at the foot of our beds, but I was too frightened to move. I climbed to the head of my bed and sat on the pillow covering the vomit. Margie came to my bed and grabbed my leg to pull me off, but as soon as she let go I scrambled back to my pillow. The next time she grabbed an arm *and* a leg and suddenly I was on the floor. Another supervisor came in with a belt and gave it to Margie. When she was finished whipping me, she took me into the shower stall and had me take off my pajamas. Then she soaked me with cold water before giving me soap to wash my body and hair. By the time I was done and dry, the maid had finished stripping the sheets from the bed and was washing the mattress.

Before I could go downstairs, Margie made me bend over the end of the bed so she could take my temperature with a rectal thermometer. Terrified that I was going to be spanked, all my muscles were tense, which didn't make Margie's job any easier.

After breakfast, I was so tired that I fell asleep under the apple tree. Indoors, I could feel the vibration of the dinner bell with my whole body, but when we were outside, I had to watch the others for cues. Asleep under the tree, I had no way to know it was time to go in. One of the other girls shook my arm to wake me up when it was time for lunch. I slowly opened my eyes and panicked because the others were marching into the dining room. The girl and I hurriedly caught up with the rest of the crowd and sat down for our meal.

Everyone got served but the girl and me, and although no words were spoken and we dared not look at each other, we both knew what was coming. Margie took the girl to punish her; I'm not sure if she was being punished for waking me up, touching me, or being late in line. Then it was my turn. When Margie was finished, I went back to sit next to the girl who had helped me. After lunch, Margie came for the girl again. She was gone for a long time, and when I finally saw her again her face was bruised and her lips swollen. She staggered as she tried to walk, doubled over in pain and trying not to cry out. She didn't look at us.

Commotion and a loud noise from the end of the dining room told us that the lunchtime excitement wasn't over yet. I tried not to turn my head but I couldn't help it. Others were looking at a boy who had diarrhea. As he got up to leave the dining room, the supervisor grabbed one of his arms and began to whip him with the belt. He had lost control of his bowels and the mess was all over the floor. The more he struggled to get away, the more he was whipped and the more he screamed. Another supervisor went to help. When they were done, one took the boy to another room while the other began pointing and grabbing some of us. Those who were selected turned and marched single file to the gym. I was taken with the second group and waited outside the closed door for my turn to be spanked. After the spankings, we all marched back to the dining room to finish lunch.

When I was about eight or nine years old, I developed bathroom problems; I had no control over my bladder. At first

I was urinating everywhere I went and getting whipped everywhere I urinated. Then I stopped urinating or having bowel movements for several days, and the spankings stopped. The new punishment was kneeling on the floor with my back straight. As with other times when the endurance punishments were used, this meant that Pat and Warren were coming — Margie didn't want visitors to see purple bruises or open sores.

I hadn't seen my parents in such a long time that I had trouble remembering who they were. *Are they going to take me home?* I wondered. No, they had come to take me to the hospital. Someone had packed a small suitcase for me. After talking with Margie for a few minutes, Pat put me in the car and we drove down the driveway. Lying in the backseat, I was lulled to sleep by the movement of the car. I barely remember Warren carrying me onto the train. Once while I was awake the conductor stopped to give me a lollipop. Pat put it in her purse, telling the conductor that I was too sick to eat anything.

Walking down the long hallway between Pat and Warren, I wondered about all the people dressed in white. I was taken to a huge room with only six beds in it and they weren't even bunk beds! Pat helped me get dressed in a pair of funny, half-made pajamas that tied in the back.

My father left, but Pat stayed while the nurses prepared me for surgery to replace the tubes connecting my kidneys to my bladder. It turned out that these tubes had never formed properly, but they had never caused any problem until now. The nurses taped my arm to a board and Pat tried to keep my attention as they started the IV. I tried not to scream for fear that I would be whipped, but the prick of the needle when it came was nothing compared to one of Margie's beatings. Pat left when the IV was in, and the nurses kept me company. One gave me a stuffed bear and read me a bedtime story, while another held my hand and massaged my arm until I fell asleep.

I had never had so much attention and I loved it, but I was scared to death of the bear. I was positive that Margie was lurking somewhere, just waiting to take it away. The arm without the IV was tied to the bed rails to keep me from pulling out the needle, so I couldn't move the bear. I tried closing my eyes and wishing it away but it didn't work. After everyone had left and the lights were off, I used my chin to move the bear away so at least I couldn't feel it touching my skin.

In the morning, Pat came back to the hospital. A few minutes after she arrived, someone came to wheel me down to the operating room. Not knowing what was happening, I was terrified. Pat tried to calm me, but my panic increased until finally one of the nurses from the night before picked me up. I lay my head on her shoulder as she rubbed my back. When I had calmed down, instead of putting me back on the bed, she carried me down the hallway. Another nurse followed along behind, wheeling the IV stand. I didn't care where they were taking me as long as I was being held and comforted.

We went into a waiting room where the nurse sat down, holding me on her lap, until the operating room was ready. I was so relaxed that I was drifting off to sleep when someone came to tell the nurse it was time for the operation.

A lot of nurses were working on me. One was trying to keep my attention as the others taped my other arm to a board. Another nurse bent my knees and placed my feet on the operating table while still another put a black wire mesh mask over my nose and mouth. A large sheet, like a wall, covered me from the chest down, and I couldn't see my body beyond it. *Is this some new punishment?* I wondered. *What have I done wrong this time?*

The more I breathed through the mask the sleepier I got. My body was getting numb but I could still see. I looked to my right and saw the mask that was supposed to put me to sleep. It was attached by a black cord that ran to a machine with a glass filled with a bubbling liquid. When the nurse who was wrapping a blood pressure cuff around my arm looked up and saw that I was awake, she quickly reached over and grabbed the mask, putting it over my face again. I breathed deeply and sank into sleep.

The next time I woke up, I was in the room with six beds. The side rails were up on my bed, making it look like a crib. Pat was leaning over, looking down at me and gently combing her fingers through my hair. She was smiling and talking to me but I didn't know what she was saying.

Unable to move, and with my arms still taped to the boards, I slept. Sometime later the nurse came in to check the tube that ran from somewhere under the sheets to a glass jar on the floor. I couldn't move either hand to lift the covers to see where the tube came from, but later, when the nurse came in to help me bathe, I saw the bandage covering my abdomen. If I had any old scars from previous beatings when I went into the hospital, either the nurses chose to ignore them or Pat satisfied them with an explanation.

Because they were afraid I would pull out the IV or tear off my bandage, the nurses kept my hands taped and fed me themselves. When the stitches and IV were finally removed, I was allowed to go into the TV room. I stood in awe next to the table with puzzles, crayons, and coloring books. I didn't know what to do with any of these things, so I spent all my time on the rocking horse in the corner. I had never seen one of those either, and I loved it. It was supported by springs and moved very slowly; even so, a nurse had to hold me when I rode.

The night before my discharge I climbed out of the crib to wander around the hallway wearing the pajamas with no bottoms. One nurse, my favorite, caught up with me, picking me up and putting my head on her shoulder. We sat down, and as she rubbed my back and rocked me, she sang me to sleep before putting me back to bed. I hadn't known that anyone but my grandmother could be so kind.

The next morning Pat was back again, and this time when she left, she took me with her. Neither my father nor any of my brothers had come to see me. As we walked down the same long hallway, me clutching my teddy bear, the nurses were all waving good-bye. I didn't want to go, but if I had to, I wanted them to come too. I watched the nurses until we rounded a corner and I couldn't see them anymore.

When we got to the street I began dragging my feet and pulling back to the door until Pat slapped me and sat me down on the car seat. I didn't move or cry on the trip back to Stoutamyre, back to Margie. Pat and Margie talked for a while before Pat left without waving good-bye to me. Margie had one of the supervisors take my things to the room upstairs while she took me to the playground. I never saw the teddy bear again. It vanished, I supposed, to the same place all the other bears and stuffed animals we had been given over the years had gone.

Life at Stoutamyre after my surgery was different in only one way: I was allowed an extra few minutes when it was my turn to go to the bathroom and the supervisor waited until I was done before opening the door.

That year I also got the mumps. Margie looked me over for fresh bruises before calling the doctor, who listened to my heart, felt my neck, and gave me a balloon. (I never had a chance to find out what the balloon was for; Margie took it from me and burst it as soon as he left.) He told Margie to move me out of the girls' sleeping area and into her sisters' living quarters on the first floor. Their spare bedroom, complete with TV and a bathroom next door, was mine for the next ten days. The maid brought a tray of food three times a day, I watched TV, and I felt like a queen until the swelling in my neck went away. I was sent back with the rest of the children as soon as I was better.

Yet I didn't recover entirely, and for a time, I was sick more and more frequently. I spent a lot of time in bed with a bucket on the floor next to me. One day I was so sick that Margie hired a nurse to stay for a few days. Late that night, my throat parched, I crept into the bathroom to get water when nobody was around, but it tasted foul and most of it came back up into the bucket before I fell asleep. I awoke to the gentle hand of the nurse patting me on my shoulder. I had fallen out of bed in my sleep. Smiling, she picked me up and put me back in bed. She hugged me and tucked me in. Margie came in and the nurse turned to walk away with her.

Pretending to be asleep, I buried my face in the covers to hide my tears. I wanted the nurse to come back and hold me again. I wanted her to be there, smiling and patting my shoulder, when I woke in the morning. I had no idea there were so many things that people who lived on the outside took for granted. Simple human kindness—a smile, a gentle hand, a warm hug, being tucked into bed, a mother's love, a kiss on the cheek, being able to enjoy having a best friend—all had been taken from me.

Both the girls' and the boys' bedrooms had a long bench for group spankings. Margie used group spankings when more than one child had done the same thing that she didn't like. For her, it was a time-saver. Four or five girls would bend over the bench, pants pulled down, hands and feet on the floor, as the supervisor moved up and down the row, spanking each one. Any child caught looking received a longer, more vigorous spanking.

Once during a group spanking I secretly watched through half-closed eyes. I saw how the girls' bottoms got red. I watched as a girl with short blonde hair moved her hand to her rear to soften the blow. Without missing a stroke, Margie removed the girl's hand and continued on with the beating, punishing her longer than the rest. I watched Margie's eyes, bright with enjoyment, her face shining with the sweat of exertion as she moved quickly up and down the row.

When the spanking was over, I quickly closed my eyes so she wouldn't see me looking. After the others had pulled their pants up and were back in bed, one girl started sobbing. It was the blonde girl who had tried to cover her bottom with her hand. I watched in horror as Margie jerked her from her bed to whip her again. It took her a while to realize that she had to stop crying before Margie would stop whipping her. By then, the skin on her bottom was broken and her legs and hand were red.

I wasn't aware that a supervisor was standing in the shadows, watching me watch the spanking. When Margie was finished with the girl, she and the supervisor moved toward me. The supervisor pushed my head down on the floor and held my arms out to the side as Margie held my feet down with one hand while whipping me with the other. I clamped my mouth shut so I wouldn't make a sound and squeezed my eyes shut so I couldn't cry, but because I had watched the other whipping, I was beaten for a long time. The scabs from my last beating cracked open and bled.

After I was back in bed and the lights were out, the blonde girl started to cry again. As she was dragged out of bed again, I could see that she had wet her pajamas. After the beating, Margie and the supervisor dragged her into the bathroom to hose her down. They beat her off and on all night.

The next day was difficult and painful for all of us. Finally, we were all standing at the foot our beds waiting for bathroom roll call. At one bunk bed, though, only one girl was standing; the other girl hadn't gotten up. At first I thought it was the blonde girl who had been beaten for so long last night. But then I saw it was one of the older girls.

We were not supposed to look as Margie stormed over to the bunk and shook the girl's shoulder roughly. Out of the corner of my eye I saw Margie lift the sheet and then quickly drop it again over the girl's face. Without bathroom roll call and with our pajamas still on, we were all taken through the dining room and outside to the gym. Later, as we were returning from the gym for a late breakfast, an unfamiliar white station wagon pulled out of the driveway. When we got back to our sleeping area the girl was gone. We never saw her again.

The blonde girl who had been beaten throughout the night survived, but had trouble walking as the supervisors brought her to the dining room to join us for our late breakfast. They had probably been cleaning her sores while we were in the gym. As she tried to sit down she screamed in pain. Obviously she had not yet learned her lesson. Margie, belt in hand, took her to another room and we didn't see her for many days. The next time we saw the girl, her face was bruised and her lips swollen and cracked. Her fingers looked like breakfast sausages, and when she shielded her eyes from the sun, I knew she had been in the dark room. She could not sit down, so she lay in the grass under the oak tree, only moving to swat the flies away from her open sores.

The girl who didn't get up after the group spanking wasn't the only child to disappear while I was at Stoutamyre. During dinnertime one day, one of the boys had an accident in his pants. As if from nowhere, rough hands lifted him from his chair, and Margie began marching him out of the dining room. Knowing what was going to happen, the boy began to yell and struggle. Sensing the commotion of the supervisors trying to subdue the boy, I turned my head a little and saw one holding him while the other tried to whip him. He was screaming the entire time, and soon several others were looking. As Margie struggled with the boy, trying to get him down on the floor, his head hit the wall and then he was still. The supervisors kept beating him for a while before they realized that he was no longer moving or crying.

I didn't have to hear to know that something was terribly wrong; the tension in the room was tangible. All the supervisors were talking at once and looked like they were mad at each other. They were still breathing hard from the struggle as they kicked the boy to make him move. Then, even though we hadn't finished our sandwiches, we were quickly herded up the stairs to the bedrooms. Through it all, the supervisors kept track of who had watched, who had seen the boy lying on the floor.

Time passed. No one called the bathroom roll; we were to stay on our beds with our clothes on. We saw Margie make a lot of phone calls from her bedroom and then go back downstairs. Unaware that one of the supervisors was hiding behind the door to our room, some of us left our beds to look out the window. We watched as a station wagon pulled up in front of the building and the maintenance man got out and walked quickly into the building. When he reappeared he was carrying the boy's heavy, motionless body. The rear door of the station wagon was open and the man laid the boy down in the back and drove away.

We all scrambled to get back in our beds, still unaware of the hidden supervisor. She stayed out of sight until Margie came to get her, then they lined us up in groups of five at the long bench. As they began the second round of group spankings, some of the girls lost control and wet their pants, both out of fear and because there had been no evening bathroom roll call. The ones who wet their pants received a third round of spankings. Luckily for me, I didn't lose control.

After Margie was finished, the girls who had wet their pants were taken into the shower stall and hosed down. It was a long, long night for Margie.

The boy who was taken away in the car never came back. Was he dead? Now, looking back, I believe that he was. Was he lucky? Well, he was finally free of Margie and wouldn't be beaten anymore.

One afternoon when we were having hot dogs at the picnic tables, three boys finished early and went to the boys' side of the playground. When I saw them playing jump rope, I leaped up without thinking and ran over to jump with them. In my excitement, I crashed into the jumper and we all fell to the ground with me on the bottom of the pile, my leg twisted under my body at an odd angle.

After spanking the three boys and sending them off with another supervisor, Margie turned to me, tearing a branch off a tree as she came. Ignoring my cries, she pulled down my pants and whipped me. When she was finished, she pulled me to my feet to go inside but I screamed in agony when I put weight on my leg. Margie had everyone march to the building, then she and the maintenance man left me alone on the playground. The other children probably thought I was going to disappear, too. Remembering my last punishment for running away I wasn't too inclined to try it again, broken leg or not. I could do nothing but sit there, looking at the clouds, wondering if Margie had forgotten me.

As the sun went down and the air began to cool, a truck with flashing lights on top came across the playground. Two men wearing white clothes examined my leg before carefully lifting me onto a stretcher for the ride to the hospital.

In the examining room, the doctor ordered X rays of my leg. No one from Stoutamyre had come to the hospital, and none of my family came to be with me. One of the nurses gave me a lollipop while we waited for the X rays. Sure enough, I left with a teddy bear and a cast from my foot almost to my hip, which kept me from bending my leg.

When I was ready to be discharged, one of the nurses sat me in an old wooden wheelchair and pushed me into the hall to wait until someone came for me. I was alone—no Margie, no Pat. Frantically, I looked around for a hiding place, but even if I'd found one, my arms weren't strong enough to move the chair. I tried to get out of the chair to crawl but couldn't do it. Then I thought of the time I had tried to run away—starvation, beatings, being tied to the chair, the dark room—and I knew that I couldn't go through that again. I had no choice but to sit and wait until someone came. It didn't occur to me to try to seek help from the hospital personnel. I had no idea how to communicate with them because all forms of communication were forbidden at Stoutamyre. Also, I didn't know that the way we were treated was not normal.

Eventually, two people wheeled me out and lifted me into the backseat of a station wagon. As we drove away, I clutched the teddy bear and watched out the window as the hospital disappeared. When we got back to Stoutamyre, I was taken upstairs to the sleeping area, where I tried to hide the teddy bear under my blanket. I pretended to sleep and waited until Margie left the room before pulling the bear out. Margie, who had been waiting around the corner, roared into the room shaking her fist. She yanked the bear out of my arms, ripped its head off, and poured the stuffing in the trashcan.

I was confined to my bed while my leg was in the cast, and one of the supervisors was assigned to watch me. She brought my meals and helped me use the bedpan. She was nice, but it was easy to see that she was scared of making a wrong move and angering Margie. As my leg healed, it began to itch terribly, and when I was alone I tried unsuccessfully to get inside the cast to scratch it. Finally, a doctor and a nurse came to take the cast off. The nurse washed the old dead skin off my leg before carefully rubbing on a soothing cream. Margie wasn't around when the nurse gave me a lollipop and another teddy bear. The nurse stayed with me for a while and rubbed my back. Her touch was so kind, so gentle, that I drifted off to sleep, only waking to plead with my eyes when she hugged me good-bye.

As soon as the nurse left, Margie came striding across the floor with long, hard steps and a sour expression on her face. As if already knowing where I had hidden the poor doomed bear, she jerked back the covers, grabbed it, and tore it to shreds.

Several days later, when I thought no one was around, I got out of bed and went to the window to watch as the maid left. As I crossed the wooden floor, I looked down into the trash can and saw a patch of fabric that had been the teddy bear. Beside it was one of the black button eyes. Sighing, I turned around to get back in bed and there was Margie—and her belt. I hadn't been spanked while the cast was on my leg, so she must have figured my leg was healed enough for her to make up for all those missed opportunities.

She grabbed me, bent me over the bed, pulled down my pajamas, and whipped me. I got down on the floor and tried to crawl away, the bandage on my leg unraveling behind me. Margie kneeled down and pushed me flat on the floor before continuing the whipping. I think she had originally come to help me downstairs for dinner, but she left without me. The next day she made me walk, slowly and painfully, with the other children to meals and to the playground.

3

Margie was a totally different person, pleasant and smiling, the day Warren came to get me. She was friendly to him and even gave me a good-bye hug when we left. Confused thoughts whirled through my head. *Why did she wrap her arms around me like that when we had always been punished for physical contact? Warren and Pat never hugged me. Why did Margie only do it when I was leaving with Warren?*

We drove from early in the morning until dark. Oh, how I hated that drive! I was only in a car a few times a year, back and forth to Stoutamyre, and I always got carsick. When Warren stopped for gas he pointed to a door with a drawing that looked like a woman on it. I never liked going to the bathroom in a restaurant or gas station because I didn't know what to do. I went inside, closing the door behind me, and stood there. I knew it was not my turn to go; Number 86 wasn't in front of me. *Should I take a chance on getting whipped for sitting on the toilet out of turn?* I *did* have to go the bathroom but decided not to risk a beating.

I went back outside, hoping Warren would tell me to "sit on the toilet." He didn't. He told me to "go to the bathroom," which, in my mind, wasn't the same thing. We got back in the car and Warren began to drive again. When was I going to be able to "sit on the toilet?" Was I supposed to sit on the toilet in the little room at the gas station—even with no Number 86 in front of me? I was terribly confused and had to go really bad. Soon I lost control and began to cry hysterically, convinced that Warren would either beat me himself or take me back to Stoutamyre to have Margie beat me. I was hyperventilating and beginning to feel like I was going to pass out.

Warren pulled over to the side of the road, shouting things I couldn't understand. He pulled my suitcase out of the back-seat and tore through it looking for something for me to wear. Crying and shaking with fear, I tried to change clothes as the traffic passed by. Slapping me the whole time, Warren roughly helped me get dressed. He put my wet clothes in a paper bag while I climbed back in the front seat.

When I finally realized that I wasn't going to get a beating like Margie would give, I relaxed. I fought unsuccessfully to keep my eyes open—no one had given me permission to go to sleep. When I awoke I was lying in the backseat, covered with a blanket. *How had that happened? Did Warren put me there?* I stayed in the back, wondering what the rules were at the place we were driving to.

It was dark when we arrived and everyone else was asleep. Warren took me to a room with pajamas laid out on the bed. He told me to change and get into bed. Good! Clear instructions on what to do! But again there was no bathroom roll call. Oh well, the bed was soft and the pillow thick with down. In the quiet of the strange room, I fell asleep as soon as my head touched the pillow.

Sometime later I awoke disoriented. I had to go to the bath-room. *I can't go looking for the toilet in this building,* I thought. *What am I going to do?* No one came. Scared and trying not to cry again, I couldn't hold it anymore. I didn't want to wet the bed, so I pulled back the covers and quietly climbed out of the bed. I stood still for a minute, waiting to feel the vibrations of footsteps on the floor but still no one came. I lifted the rug by the bed, urinated on the floor, and covered the puddle with the rug. Feeling much better, I climbed back into bed and went to sleep.

I woke to bright sunlight, the strong smell of urine, and a teenage boy standing in the doorway. "Pe-e-w," he said, rolling his eyes and holding his nose as he slammed the door. I could feel each muscle in my body tighten at the thought of what would come next. I was too afraid to move. No one came to tell me to get out of bed, so I lay there until the door opened again.

This time it was Pat. She enjoyed smacking me just like Margie. I tried not to cry when she looked right at the rug covering the puddle. I thought I had hidden it so well! How did she find it?

Pat motioned for me to get out of bed, took me into the bathroom, and motioned again for me to sit on the toilet. She returned a few minutes later with clean clothes and turned the water on in the—*What was that thing? Was I supposed to get in it? I had forgotten what a bath was. Where was the liquid soap?* Not knowing what to do, I just sat there in the tub until Pat came back to help me get dressed.

Boys were everywhere downstairs—sitting on the sofa, the floor, and chairs. I knew that girls were not supposed to be near boys, but I couldn't find a way to avoid them. Ignoring my distress, Pat told me that *these* boys were my "brothers." Since I had no concept of family relationships, the word meant nothing to me. Everyone was talking but I couldn't understand what anyone was saying. I assumed that my brothers—all six of them—lived in this place. Why then were they not whipped for talking and laughing and running through the building?

I vaguely recognized some of them—Mark, Dan, Paul, and Peter—but there were two I had never seen before. I later found out that two brothers, Rick and Bill, had been born while I was at Stoutamyre.

One of the boys opened the door and a little hairy monster ran across the floor, tongue hanging and tail wagging. I sat frozen, afraid to move as it licked my leg—I had never seen a dog before. One of the boys came over to the animal and reached down to pet it, motioning for me to do the same. I was so confused. Neither Pat nor Warren had told me to move so I sat, ramrod straight and terrified, as the dog licked me until Pat took the dog back outside. When no one was looking, I tried to wipe the slime from my leg.

Staying at Pat and Warren's house was not easy. Not knowing when to go to the bathroom wasn't the only problem. At mealtimes, the boys made fun of me, calling me a robot, whatever that was. I knew how I was supposed to sit at Stoutamyre and tried to do the same, but there were no black lines on the floor to put the chair legs on.

"Stop it!" Pat said. *Stop what? What was I doing wrong?*

"Come on, Anne, relax!" said one brother. *What did that mean? And how was I supposed to do it?*

One brother told me to eat like he did, so I began copying him. I found that if I copied my brothers, I didn't get into as much trouble.

Copying my brothers didn't work when it came to clothing. I had to wear dresses, and my six brothers each wore pants. When wearing dresses, I couldn't sit like the boys did; I had to keep my knees together. I wanted to wear pants like they did so I could sit like them.

Once, at the neighborhood park, other children came to play while I was in the sandbox. They wanted me to play a game called "tag" but I didn't know how to play. Some were laughing and throwing sand on my legs and one girl tapped me to be "it." I had never been touched like that. Confused and frightened, I ran and hid behind a tree until one of my brothers came and told me to go inside.

I started to shake as I walked in the house. I knew I was in trouble but didn't know why. Was Margie going to appear from behind a door to beat me? Pat took me by the hand up to my room and beat me with a hairbrush. Later, I watched out the window as the other children played, chasing and touching each other. I couldn't understand why they weren't punished too.

During the two weeks of the visit, when Pat and Warren went shopping, I was left at home with my brothers. They liked to play ball and hide-and-seek and watch television. Once they pulled me outside to play. I didn't know what to do when one brother threw the ball to me. Girls weren't allowed to play with boys! I kept my hands to my sides and moved my head a little. Wham! The ball hit me in the face, bloodying my nose. Frightened, the boys rushed me into the house and made me sit with my head tilted back to stop the bleeding while they cleaned me up. Later, when Pat and Warren came home, they asked the boys about my swollen lips. One of the boys pantomimed falling down the stairs. Then I was scolded for falling and told to stay away from the basement stairs. I was confused.

When Pat and Warren left the room, one brother accused the other brother, saying he had lied. *Lied?* I could speechread this word, but I didn't know what it meant.

At the end of the two weeks it was time for the long drive back to Stoutamyre. This time I didn't wet the car seat because when Warren stopped at the restaurant and told me to go to the bathroom, I made sure the door was locked so I could use the toilet. It had taken two weeks, but finally I had figured out what he meant. Why hadn't I thought of it before?

It took a while to get back into the routine at school. Pat scolded me for behaving the way that had been beaten into me at Stoutamyre, and Margie beat me for behaving the way Pat wanted me to while at home. The first time I tried eating like my brothers had taught me, Margie was right there, shoving my face into my plate of food. I used the toilet when I needed to, and got a fresh batch of bruises for it. I tried to play tag, tapping a boy and running to a tree but I got caught, whipped, and sent to the room with no lights. I had a hard time understanding how life in the two worlds could be so different.

Sometimes I wasn't able to go to Warren's house for vacation. Most of the other children would be gone, leaving only a few of us at Stoutamyre. Those were the best times; Margie would be gone, leaving another supervisor in charge. When Margie wasn't there, the difference in the supervisor was dramatic. She read stories at bedtime and pushed us on the swings. We never entirely trusted the change, though, so we were still careful.

There were times, wonderful times, when my grandmother came to visit, even though Pat didn't approve. Margie would bring me into the waiting room, and my grandmother would be there, standing with her arms open wide and smiling warmly, but I was not allowed to run to her. Instead I would walk across the room slowly, showing no emotion, and I would stand stiffly and allow her to hug me. My grandmother always seemed to be in a hurry to get me away from Stoutamyre and never took any time to talk to Margie.

Probably because I was preoccupied with basking in my grandmother's affection when I was with her, I didn't wonder why my grandfather never came to visit. I didn't even think about why he wasn't there when I went home with my grandmother during school vacations. I found out later that he had died, but my grandmother didn't want to go through the pain of explaining to me that he had died and what dying meant; it was easier for her just to avoid the subject.

As much as I enjoyed seeing my grandmother, it was as difficult to adjust to being off schedule at her home as at Pat's. But my grandmother never spanked or yelled at me. She gave me lots of hugs and told me she loved me, but I didn't understand what she was saying. In the evenings my grandmother pulled me close while we watched TV and at bedtime she read me stories. She took me to the park and once to the zoo. I was terrified because I had never seen any of the animals before. When we came to the polar bear exhibit, I hid my face!

Mealtimes at my grandmother's home in New Jersey were just as confusing as at Pat and Warren's. With no lines on the floor, where were the chair legs supposed to go so I could be served? But I was served anyway, and told that I could eat after the grace was said. I ate the way I was taught at Stoutamyre, with my back straight, not bending my head to look at my food, bringing my food up to my mouth with my fork. Sometimes my grandmother gently corrected me and other times she ignored what must have seemed like strange habits. I didn't have to eat everything if I wasn't hungry, and I could have seconds if I wanted them.

At my grandmother's house I was never spanked for my accidents on the floor in the night. Whenever it happened, though, I still stood at the foot of the bed, shaking, sure that she would come after me with a belt. Instead, my grandmother would clean the messes herself. Even if I stayed in the bathroom too long or looked around the house as though I had freedom, I was never spanked.

In the mornings she woke me up with a kiss, laid out my toothbrush, and helped me with the toothpaste, because I didn't know how to use the tube. After breakfast we would go to the park or to visit relatives. In my grandmother's world it was okay for boys and girls to play together. Once, she took me to an animated cartoon movie and bought me popcorn, a sweet drink, and ice cream. I had never had any of these foods before, and I became very sick.

Margie didn't like my grandmother, and the feeling was clearly mutual. She left as quickly as possible after bringing me back to Stoutamyre. After she left, Margie dragged me by the hair, my feet barely touching the floor, to my bed. What had I done wrong? I needed to know so I could avoid being dragged by my hair again.

Years later I learned that after that particular visit, my grandmother threatened to take Pat to court to get custody of me. Pat refused and contacted the police to take out a restraining order against my grandmother. She told Margie never to allow my grandmother on the property again, and Margie was more than happy to honor her wishes. I didn't see my grandmother again for several years.

The longer I was at Stoutamyre, the more I feared Margie and the other supervisors. Whenever they came near me, even if I wasn't the intended victim, I closed my eyes and tensed my muscles to prepare for the blow that *might* come for no apparent reason. I focused all my energy on my next move, and what I was to do (or not to do) next. I had little time to daydream about my grandmother coming to visit or about what it would be like to be somewhere else. My world was very small, and surviving in it was my goal. I was careful with every move I made, whether in the dining room, the sleeping area, or on the playground. I was careful to monitor my breathing and to be sure the expression on my face didn't change. And I always was aware of where my arms and legs were. Concentrating on every move kept me from being bored.

Most of the time, however, despite my efforts, I couldn't help getting beaten. Either I made a mistake and did something that was against Margie's rules, or she added a new rule that I hadn't learned yet.

I trained myself to avoid coughing. If I held in my stomach just so, took small breaths, and cleared my throat quietly, I could minimize coughing spells when I had a cold. But I never learned to hide a sneeze, and the noise brought Margie running.

Margie knew that I wasn't stupid, although I played stupid at times and got away with it. One day I didn't feel like eating supper, so I pretended that I didn't know my chair legs were not lined up properly so I could skip the meal. I learned on other days that if I ate really fast I would be able to clean my plate before feeling full. Then later, on the playground, I would get as far away as I could from the outside supervisor and, with my back to her, throw up from eating too much. Then I spread the regurgitated food around in the dirt with my foot, leaving no evidence of my crime.

When we were on the playground, I comforted myself by rocking back and forth. I knew I would be whipped for rocking in the dining room or the sleeping area. On one occasion while we were lined up I forgot where I was and started rocking from side to side. The whipping I received taught me to be more careful of where I rocked.

The need to reach out, to find comfort in some kind of human contact, was overwhelming. Even though it was forbidden, sometimes I tried to communicate with others through my body language. Most either did not understand or were afraid to respond, but one girl seemed more like me. It was the same girl who had woken me up when I fell asleep under the tree. I decided that she would be my secret friend. Even though I didn't know the word or its meaning, I knew the feeling of "sameness" or closeness that I felt toward her.

Our communication was minimal, done mostly with our eyes. For example, I would move my eyes back and forth really fast if a supervisor was coming and she would do the same. We dared not make a game of it, for fear of being whipped. We tried to watch each other from the corners of our eyes to give emotional support. Some of the others who tried to communicate with their eyes gave up; they were too afraid of getting caught.

One night while my secret friend was being whipped, I lay in my bed pretending to be asleep. As she lay there trying not to move, I could feel the stinging pain going through her body every time the belt made contact with her skin. I saw the expression on her face as she tensed every muscle and tried not to make a sound. I tried to will her to be strong and not cry out because I knew the beating would continue even longer.

Sometimes after a whipping, a child would be left in bed the next day. On those days the maid always spent extra time with that child when Margie was otherwise occupied. She cleaned and treated our wounded bottoms and always finished her gentle treatment with a hug. I lived for those hugs. One day Margie came in and caught the maid hugging a child and, with poison in her eyes, ordered the woman to leave the room. After whipping the child who was being hugged, Margie stormed out. We never saw that maid again. A few days later we had a new maid: a stiff, unfeeling woman who did exactly as she was told.

I remember a time when nobody received any beatings; we all knew something was going to happen. It turned out that Margie had planned an open house.

The day before the open house was devoted to cleaning the place from top to bottom. Cleaning wasn't a part of our normal routine, so Margie had problems keeping everyone organized— but company was coming, so there were no beatings. Some of the children washed the walls, windows, and floors; my job was to clean the stairway from the sleeping area to the dining room. With a bucket of water and a rag I washed each wooden step then dried it with another cloth. Then I used a cloth to polish the railing and made sure there were no marks on the floor. It took me the whole day to clean the stairs.

While Margie made sure that the inside was clean, the maintenance man took care of the outside, mowing the lawn, neatly trimming the hedges, and sweeping the walkways. Someone put flowers on the windowsills.

The day of the open house dawned warm and sunny. Margie had on one of her good dresses. After breakfast, children with no visible wounds or bruises were sent to the playground with a supervisor. The children whose bruises had not healed were put in a back room where they would not be seen. Parents and people from Bridgewater came, and everyone was very impressed with the cleanliness of the Stoutamyre School for Special Education and the care its students received. That day we were all treated nicely no matter how we acted. I knew that all infractions were being stored in Margie's memory and would be recalled at the end of the day. But any punishments were put on hold until after everyone left.

The supervisors were on hand to conduct tours and answer questions, and the visitors were free to walk all over the property. Some tried to talk to us but we knew better than to try to say anything. The visitors, thinking we were all retarded, probably thought we were shy. One woman walked up to me, smiling, and patted me on the cheek. She talked for a while but I didn't know what she was saying, not that I would have dared trying to communicate even had I understood her. She finally gave up and walked away.

Margie received a lot of gifts that day. Farmers brought watermelons and several families brought candy. Others brought ice cream and stuffed animals. Several people brought used bicycles and encouraged some of the boys to try to ride, but no one knew how.

Pat and Warren were there and were treated like royalty. When they arrived, Pat and Margie hugged like long-lost friends. At the time I couldn't comprehend what all this hugging was for. They stood together, arms around each other, smiling at me. While Pat and Warren were there, Margie gave me candy and hugged me every chance she got. But as soon as they were gone everything was taken away and Margie pushed me around as if she regretted ever hugging me.

When the open house was over, so was our fun. Margie was busy with the other supervisors, taking away anything we had been given. If anyone tried to hide something or pretend they had not been given something, they were whipped. We all had to throw our teddy bears into large bags while the maintenance man put the bikes in the storage building. Only the food was not thrown away. I gave my teddy bear back without crying and did not get whipped that day.

All I knew at Stoutamyre was pain and fear, and I saw a lot of things that a young child shouldn't have seen. I saw others being punished and Margie's flushed face and evil expression as she tightened up to whip us. I saw the faces of the other children as they suffered. I saw how they tried to control their screams and hold back the tears. I saw how some tried to run away from Margie or fight back. I saw when some of them disappeared. No one could win. No one could overpower Margie. She was everywhere, ready to attack any minute, and the vibration of her feet on the floor was enough to send chills up my spine.

Much later, after I had left and had learned to communicate with those around me, I told my story to Pat and Warren but they didn't believe me. They accused me of lying, and after a while I began to believe them. It was all too horrible to be true. In time I almost convinced myself that none of it had ever happened.

4

The year was about 1965. I say "about" because we had no access to calendars and wouldn't have known what to do with them if we had them. It was springtime, with the last residue of the final snow of the season melting in the shady areas of Stoutamyre's grounds and the trees just beginning to show signs of pale green. After breakfast one morning, we were all taken to the gym. Because Margie didn't allow communication between the supervisors and the children—with the exception of gesturing or punishment—no one knew what was going to happen. Any change from our day-in, day-out routine was unnerving and caused my adrenaline level to soar.

Some of the children were directed to take seats around a large table in the middle of the gym. (I recognized the table as the one that had always been folded against a wall, out of the way. Now I know that it was a Ping-Pong table that none of the children had ever used.) A man wearing a suit appeared to be in charge and was passing out pencils and paper. Several women were assigned to help the children fill in the space beside the word "name."

A slim woman with fair skin and long, straight brown hair sat down beside me. First she made sure that I had Number 87 on the correct line then smiled reassuringly as she held up a picture of a red square. From a selection of pictures in front of me she found a red square and held it up as a way of explaining what was expected of me. Then she found a picture of a blue triangle, showed it to me and waited. I quickly found the matching picture in my pile and held it up. She smiled and made a mark on her paper. Next she showed me a picture of two balls. I looked at my pictures and found one that matched the one she was holding. "Very good," she said, still smiling. After matching a few more sets of pictures, she cleared the table and put the pictures in a box beside her. After making sure that I was watching her, she hit the table three times with the palm of her hand and waited expectantly. I hit the table three times. She nodded her head three times and I did the same. Then she brought out a puzzle board that held a triangle, square, circle, and rectangle, and dumped the pieces on the table before pushing the empty board to me. I picked up each piece, and looked at it briefly before putting it in the correct hole. Turning the puzzle around, she had me repeat the process.

I was having fun until she started to make sounds. With her face and her body language, she encouraged me to repeat the vowel sounds but I sat mute, frozen in my chair. I looked around the room and saw Margie in one corner, rocking in a rocking chair. The message in her eyes was crystal clear; I was not allowed to use my voice. The fun was over. After several futile attempts the woman gave up and packed her materials, letting me know it was time to leave. I was taken outside and another child was led in. I was afraid I would be whipped when all the testers left, but I wasn't.

For the next several days Margie stayed out of sight more than usual, and in the evenings we could see her hard at work at her desk with stacks of folders beside her. A month or so later, Pat and Warren came to pick me up. They were tense and spent a long time talking to Margie. Then everything was rush,

rush, rush, as Warren loaded my suitcase in the car. Margie wasn't smiling and she didn't hug me good-bye as I left. The ride home was the same as other times. I had no way of knowing that I would not be going back.

By summertime, I still wasn't used to being around the boys, whom I barely remembered from previous visits. My oldest brother Mark was home for a short time before going to Vietnam. Dan, the next oldest, had a paper route and so did my twin brother, Peter. Paul had a part-time job at a hamburger place. Pat and Warren's two young sons, Rick and Bill, were nine and seven years old.

Rick and Bill often invited me to their room to play with their G.I. Joe dolls and little plastic army men, but I was very confused. According to Stoutamyre rules I wasn't allowed to play with boys. Those rules seemed suspended here though, so I went. But when Pat came upstairs, carrying a basket full of clean laundry, I jumped up so fast that I knocked over all the men on the "good" side of the fort the boys had built. One brother got mad and started yelling, but Pat told him to be nice to me. My other brothers were uneasy around me and avoided me whenever possible. In a very real sense we were strangers, and they had no idea how to act any more than I did. I was a new ingredient in the family soup.

My family had a difficult time adjusting to the behaviors I had been taught at Stoutamyre. My brothers, who continued to make fun of my table manners, went wild the day I spilled my milk and tried to lick it up off the table. Pat's slap across my ear made me jump. *What did I do wrong this time?* I wondered. No one seemed to understand that I was only doing what I had been taught to do for five years, and I had no way of explaining. My odd behaviors only reinforced Pat's belief that I was retarded.

I continued to try to follow Margie's rule of only going to the bathroom when I was told to go. It was difficult to get used to not going immediately after someone else. In the house, if no one told me to go, I went on the floor in my room or in the basement. When I was told to go, I used the toilet, but I hurried to finish and was always surprised when there was no one outside the door timing me. If I was outside and had to go, I hid in the bushes where no one could see, rather than going inside. Occasionally I had accidents in my pants. Sometimes I got caught before I could change my clothes and those times I was whipped by Pat. Then when Warren got home and Pat told him, he had his turn whipping me.

When I began my stay at home, with no bathroom roll call before bedtime, I often went on the floor in the night. One morning Pat came in and, catching the odor, closed and locked my bedroom door. She searched on her hands and knees until she found where I had hidden the solid stool under the bed, thinking no one would find it there. She grabbed my hairbrush off the dresser, pulled down my pants, and whipped me. When she was finished and I had pulled my pants back up, I moved toward the door to leave the room, but the door was locked and I didn't know how to unlock it. For some reason that infuriated Pat, and she grabbed me and began beating me again, yelling and screaming. When she was done she left me alone in my room with the door shut.

Later that evening Warren came in with a belt. I was scared and tried to get away as he chased me around the small room. Hearing the commotion, Pat walked in, closing the door behind her just as he caught me. Between them they flipped me over on the bed and Pat sat on my back while my father pulled down my pants and whipped me. The beating seemed to go on forever, and every time my father stopped, Pat urged him on. I could see her telling him, "Give her more, Warren! Teach her a lesson!" I cleaned up the mess under the bed when they were done. Pat made me sit on the toilet for a long time but I didn't have to go, then I was sent to bed without dinner.

Many nights I was sent to my room after being whipped for doing or not doing something, but I seldom knew why. The rules were different here and I had yet to learn them. I never saw any of my brothers whipped for anything. Why were they treated so differently? They laughed, talked, and showed emotions but were never punished. They fought with each other, ran through the house, and played, and neither Pat nor Warren ever took a belt to their bottoms.

Without a fence around the yard I had no idea where my boundaries were, and no one showed me. They just assumed that I would know where our yard ended and the neighbors' began. Instead of park benches to sit on or an oak tree to lie under, there were bikes and scooters, but no one took the time to teach me how to ride.

When I tried to play with the other children in the neighborhood, they laughed at me, making faces and calling me retarded. When a girl's stolen bike was found on a neighbor's property, I was blamed even though I didn't know how to cross the street. It was easy for my brothers and the other children to blame me for their accidents, carelessness, and mischief once they realized that I couldn't talk. At a picnic with some neighbors, my brothers and the other children took great delight in teasing me. They threw french fries at me, and when Pat wasn't looking, smeared ketchup all over the table and dumped the salt shaker on my plate, giggling all the while. I watched them, bewildered, wondering what in the world they were doing. When Pat came out and saw the mess, they told her I had done it. Pat pulled me up from my seat and slapped me in front of everyone before sending me to my room. Later I looked out my window and saw the children staring up at me, laughing.

Life at Pat and Warren's house (it was hardly my home) was even more confusing than at Stoutamyre. At least with Margie I could eventually figure out why I had been punished. The rules there, harsh as they were, applied to almost everyone. At Pat and Warren's house the rules were still unclear. And the boys seemed to have a different set of rules than I did.

Bedtime was as difficult as suppertime. I was always pushed roughly aside when I walked too closely behind my brothers going up the stairs after supper. Why? I had always marched closely behind someone when going up to the sleeping area to get ready for bed. When I got to my bedroom, I didn't dare change clothes until I had been told to do so. I stood at the foot of my bed, waiting for Pat to come in and give me the signal to put on my pajamas.

One night my room was dark when I got there, and I didn't know how to turn on the light. I stood in the dark, waiting for Pat to come. Two of my brothers stood in the doorway to my room laughing and pointing at me for a while. When they left, they locked the door to my room from the inside and closed it behind them. My legs were tired and I was sleepy so I sat on the edge of the bed, planning to get up fast when Pat walked in. No one ever came, and I fell asleep in my clothes.

The next morning I changed quickly and sat back on the bed to wait. Pat came to get me every morning. After five years of being directed in every move I was unable to decide on my own when to go to the bathroom, brush my teeth, or go downstairs. After a while, when no one came, I tried to peek out the door to see if anyone was around and discovered that the door was still locked. I had no idea how to unlock it, and I had to go to the bathroom. I held it as long as I could, waiting for Pat to come. Just when I thought I would have to go on the floor, the doorknob moved, but the door didn't open. Pat pounded on the door, yelling something. I couldn't make out the words, but I knew I would be whipped if I didn't open the door, and in my fear, I wet my pajamas. In a few minutes I saw one of my brothers at the bedroom window motioning for me to let him in. I pushed up the window and he climbed in, unlocked the door, and left as Pat came in with the belt. The wet pajama bottoms added fuel to her fury as she whipped me. Later, in pain and total confusion, I tried to figure out if I was whipped for opening the window, not opening the door, or wetting myself.

Eventually Pat tired of telling me what to do and tried to make me do things for myself. Only after several weeks was I able to get undressed and go to bed without being told, and even then I always slept facing the door, ready to sit up fast if someone came in the room, unwilling to let anyone catch me sleeping without permission. Five years of painful lessons had created habits that were difficult to break. Pat and Warren perceived my adherence to Margie's rules to be behavior problems, which led to a lot of punishments, and they were losing patience with me.

If Pat and Warren had a clue that Stoutamyre was not a school but rather an institution (in the worst sense), they never let me know. Many years I tried to tell Pat that at Stoutamyre there were no classes, no homework, and no lessons except learning to keep still, keep quiet, and avoid Margie's rage. She responded by telling me that I had been Margie's favorite student. Pat and Warren had sent me away to school so I could learn how to be "normal," so they were angry when the girl who came back was a robot, a walking zombie. At eleven years old, after five years at a "school," and living in a large family, I still did not know my name.

5

I had only been living with Pat and Warren for a short time when they moved to Morristown, Pennsylvania. Warren was an engineer, and his new promotion let him travel a great deal. He planned it that way—it was easier to be away from home on a business trip than to face Pat's complaining. Warren and Pat had lots of communication problems but instead of trying to work them out, he let her take control of the household.

I could tell that Pat didn't want me living with her and Warren and my brothers, and she spent a lot of time trying to find a way to get me out of the house again. She didn't like my grandmother, so she didn't want me living there either, for that would make my grandmother happy. Pat wanted me to go somewhere else, a place where she wouldn't have to see me or think about me. We had only been living in Pennsylvania for about six months when I walked into my room and found Pat packing my suitcase.

The ride to the second institution was short, not even long enough for me to get carsick. After turning off the main road onto a long, winding, tree-lined road, Warren pulled up in front of a tall, spiked black iron fence surrounding several buildings clustered together. The closest building was castle-like, made of stone, and had a huge double door in front. A plaque on the front door read, "St. Mary's of Providence Center," and Pat read it loudly so I could hear her.

The right half of the heavy arched door opened and a woman dressed all in black, with even her head covered, stood there smiling widely. I had never seen a nun before. I backed up in fear, trying to hide behind Warren. Was this Margie, trying to trick me by dressing in all black? Had she missed her "favorite student" so much that she came here to this strange place to whip me? Were there not enough children at Stoutamyre to beat?

The woman, Sister Mary Patricia, walked toward me, still smiling, and reached out her hand to take mine. When I wouldn't take her hand, Pat took me by the arm and put my hand in the nun's hand. We walked through a large reception area with marble floors and antique furniture, through another set of double doors on the left, and on to the wide, curving wooden stairs that led to the bedrooms. The nun talked to me in soothing tones as she held my hand and walked with me up the stairs. Even though I couldn't hear the words, I knew the tone was similar to that used by the nurse and the maid at Stoutamyre.

As we walked, I lay my other hand on the polished stair rail, but it was so wide that my hand did not reach all the way across. Another child might have seen that stair rail as a huge temptation to slide, but I had never learned that fine delight of childhood.

Each bedroom was large, with its own bathroom. Each bathroom had five toilets in individual stalls, and one bathroom had a large, white, claw-footed tub. Across from the toilets was a row of sinks. The first and second bedrooms each had ten regular beds—not bunk beds—and the third had five. A towel and a washcloth lay over the rail at the end of each bed and pajamas were folded neatly under the pillow. Near the head of each bed was a hook holding a robe and underneath were slippers. At the back of the bedroom, built into the wall, were drawers with words on them. I later learned that these words were names and that each student had one.

After a tour of the bedrooms, we turned to go back downstairs. To the rear of the downstairs hall was another spiral staircase which led to an area upstairs that may have been for the nuns' personal use. Towards the front of the building, a set of double doors led to the dining room. Amazingly, the tables here were lined up in two rows of four tables, each with four chairs, a tablecloth, and a centerpiece!

Opposite the dining room was the infirmary. On one wall was a locked white metal cabinet with a glass front, filled with medicines, Q-tips, bandages, and rubbing alcohol. Taped to the front was a schedule of who got what medicine and when. The small desk in one corner held each girl's medical records. In the other corner was an examination table.

The room we had walked through to get to the stairs was a playroom with a television, lots of couches, a piano, a closet filled with board games, and an area for arts and crafts. On a small table near the couches was a statue of the Virgin Mary dressed in a blue robe, her hands open and her head bent down, as though she were looking at me. She had a large, red, shining heart in her chest and a crushed snake under her bare feet. On the wall behind her was a mural of winged angels blowing trumpets. The bright afternoon sun shown through the windows along the other side. Another section of this room had lockers filled with roller skates, balls, bats, Frisbees, a volleyball, a folded Ping-Pong table, and assorted lawn games.

Next to the front entrance was a conference room. The walls were paneled halfway up from the floor and the upper half was painted light green. The windows were long and narrow. On one side were built-in bookcases filled with books written by Dickens and Emerson and others. At the rear of this room was Sister Mary Patricia's office. I found out later that she was the mother superior.

From the playroom we could walk to a sidewalk that branched in three directions. The walkway to the left led to a playground with swings, a rocking horse, monkey bars, and a shed where the bicycles were stored. The center sidewalk led to the Catholic church where Mass was held every Sunday. The sidewalk to the right led to the school building, the library, the gymnasium, and to a nature area with a pond. From the other side of the church a sidewalk led to the nuns' sleeping quarters.

Another door led from the playground into the dining room, and twenty-five girls were seated, ready for dinner, when we entered. The nun who had been holding my hand motioned for me to sit in an empty chair and I immediately looked behind it for the line on which to place my chair legs. I was disappointed when I didn't find it, certain that I wouldn't be served a meal. The nun came over, helped push my chair closer to the table, and put a napkin on my lap. Then she came back and set a steaming plate of good-smelling food in front of me.

Without a hug or even a handshake, Pat and Warren waved as they turned to leave. Preoccupied with watching how the other girls ate, I waved a little but barely noticed as they left. Here there appeared to be no rules about bringing your fork to your mouth or keeping your back rigid, but just to be sure, I sat the way I had been taught. While waiting for everyone else to finish their dinner, I saw two women in white outfits just like the cooks at Stoutamyre wore. Even though their faces and hair color were different, because of the clothes I thought they were the same cooks. They looked at me and smiled. It was a long time before I realized that they were not the same women.

We left the dining room single file and went upstairs to the bedrooms where we changed into pajamas, robes, and slippers.

My own flannel Mickey Mouse pajamas had magically appeared under the pillow on the bed that was to be mine. Then we went back downstairs to the playroom, where the other girls settled in to watch TV, play board games, or read. I was afraid to do anything for fear of getting whipped.

I had very little contact with the other girls for quite a while. They knew how to laugh and cry, but I had repressed my emotions for so many years that I had forgotten how. One girl even asked the sisters why I never cried. The other girls had manners and knew how to ask for what they wanted. They knew to answer when their names were called, and I wasn't even sure I had a name. For a while I thought my name might be "Aye," because that was a sound that Pat yelled very loudly sometimes. Before, at Stoutamyre, I had been Number 87, but here no one used numbers in that way.

Soon after my arrival at St. Mary's, I was assigned a tutor who taught me that my name was Anne. At first I thought it was a game. I couldn't understand how I had received my name. *How can I have something I cannot see*, I wondered. *What is a name, anyway? What color is it? How long do I get to keep it?* When I tried to say my name, it was no different than saying the letter "n." I was confused for a long time before I began to understand that *I* was Anne.

My tutor taught me the written alphabet and how to count, but she had a difficult time trying to get me to talk. The memories of beatings for making noises with my mouth were so strong that I wouldn't even attempt to make a sound. I learned to love writing and drawing, however, and was writing short sentences long before I could say words that anyone could understand.

The sisters arranged for Sister Martha to give me a complete physical. She wasn't a doctor, but probably a nurse practitioner, and she was very good at getting me to relax. She tried to make a game of it and hugged me after we completed each part of the examination. When I had to take my shirt off so she could listen to my heart, she tickled me to make me laugh. My whole body tensed and I pulled away. When she saw my fear, she gave me a quick hug and a smile. When she was finished, she told me that I was good, gave me a candy bar, and sent me to the playground with Sister Mary. (Several of the nuns were named Sister Mary, but this particular one was my favorite!) Suspecting that something was wrong with my hearing, Sister Martha arranged for me to see a specialist.

When I was at Stoutamyre, I didn't know that my hearing was any different than anyone else's. I often wondered how Margie knew when I got out of my bed to see what was going on in the other room. How did she know when I got up in the middle of the night to go to the bathroom, even though I checked to make sure her eyes were closed? How did she find me when I crawled under the bed to hide from her to avoid a beating? I didn't realize that she could hear me. I thought that if *I* couldn't hear what I was doing, then *she* couldn't either.

In addition to a complete physical, every girl was given IQ and neurological examinations. Pat, fearing that the nuns would think less of her, had given them very little information. But the nuns were smart, well-educated teachers and could tell that I hadn't come from a normal environment. From the way I responded to the world around me, they suspected abuse and neglect. Their evaluations convinced the sisters that I wasn't retarded, and they proceeded to give me the care and treatment I needed.

After the visit with the second specialist, in an attempt to lessen my feelings of difference, the sisters told me that I had "a little hearing problem" and that it was no big deal. They provided me with my first hearing aid and worked hard to help me overcome the fear of wearing it. The mold went in my right ear and was attached by a cord to a small box that clipped onto my clothes. Sister Mary adjusted the volume knob and suddenly I heard a door closing behind me. I whirled around, pointing at the sound, and Sister Mary smiled and hugged me.

With my hearing aid, I heard birds chirping, chairs moving, people walking, and voices all around. So this was what I had been missing! After a lifetime of virtual silence, the new noises were frightening at first and gave me headaches if I wore the hearing aid for more than a few hours. But as my body and mind adjusted to the new sensation, I was able to extend the time. In the beginning I spent a lot of time trying to locate the source of sounds and was often distracted from what I was doing. But the nuns did not punish me for being distracted; they were so excited with the success of the hearing aid that they allowed me plenty of time to adjust.

I was scheduled for speech therapy with a nun who had incredible patience. She made it her job to help me overcome some of my habits from Stoutamyre. As she got more and more firm with me during the speech lesson, I finally spoke my first word: "box." She put an empty box on the table and said the word. Then she took my hand and placed my fingers on the side of her throat as she said, "Box" again. She took her fingers from her throat and put them on my own. "B . . . b . . . b . . . ah . . . ah . . . ah . . . ks," I managed to say, and then put it all together. Then she did the same with my name. Then I was to repeat her name, Sister Mary. I stood in front of her, trembling—in fear, not excitement. Was this a trick? Would I be whipped for speaking? But no, Sister Mary wouldn't be smiling so widely and praising me if she were going to whip me.

I hadn't received any real punishment since arriving at St. Mary's. Occasionally one of the nuns would slap my hand if I touched something I wasn't supposed to or if I took something that didn't belong to me. The most common punishment was to have privileges taken away. The only spankings I ever saw were one or two swats on the rear, using bare hands only, and the girl always had her clothes on. And if I happened to see the girl being punished, I wasn't whipped for watching. There were no belts or whips, no boards with holes, no tables with straps. There was no dark room without any lights or windows. The worst punishment was being made to stand in the corner, unable to watch cartoons. No one was ever made to go without meals. If anyone was punished, the sister explained why. As mild as the punishments were, the girls still hated them and worked hard to avoid earning them.

My biggest problem was a complete lack of social skills. I just didn't fit in. I was learning to speak, but my speech was still slow, broken, and halting. I was still nervous and afraid of many things and the other girls laughed at me and called me a baby when I wet my pants. I had a hard time adjusting to having unlimited bathroom privileges. I took things that belonged to the other girls; I had no concept of *yours, mine, ours,* or *theirs* because I had never had any of my own possessions.

Some of the other girls had hearing problems and others were slow learners. Some seemed to have no disabilities, while others liked to rock back and forth like I did, which was all right—at St. Mary's rocking was acceptable. When I arrived there were already some cliques, but my behaviors were so different than those of most of the girls that I never seemed to fit in. In addition, I was hyperactive, for which I took medication.

The sisters at St. Mary's gave me the first birthday party that I remember, complete with singing, cake, and gifts. I think I was eleven. Since Pat had not given them my birth date, they chose to celebrate it in October; I remember because on the wall calendar the name of the month began with a big *O*. When I blew out the candles everyone clapped and cheered, and all the nuns hugged me. I was very confused the next month when we were celebrating the November birthdays. I wanted to be the one blowing out the candles and getting hugs from the sisters.

All the other girls went to different classes depending on their grade. Rather than joining them, I had classes with the mother superior. Soon, though, I was able to move into a class with four other girls. We studied arithmetic, reading, writing, and spelling. I learned to add and subtract and my reading improved. It wasn't long before I was getting 100 percent on my homework and tests and earning chips as rewards. The chips were tokens we could use to "buy" candy or soft drinks or time for walks or movies with the nuns. I had my own chip bank and took great pride in earning as many as I could. I saved my chips for extra time with Sister Mary.

The nuns were very close to all of us. I had seen enough television by this time to begin to understand what a family was supposed to be like, and they seemed to me to act the way a mother should. The sisters were generous with affection and, starved for it as I was, I never could seem to get enough. Sister Mary Patricia was my favorite, and I loved to lay my head on her lap while she read to me. Even though chronologically I was nearly a teenager, the sisters realized that emotionally I was still quite young, and they nourished that young child in me with their tender care.

Time rolled on, and soon it was Christmas. Before we were sent home for the holidays, we had a Christmas party in the gym complete with Santa Claus and gifts. At first I thought we were lining up for a spanking, and when it was my turn to go to the large, smiling man in the red suit I was so terrified that I could barely walk. One of the sisters lifted me to his lap and I quickly scrambled to get off again, but not before Santa gave me a gift. I sat down and turned the package over in my hands, not knowing what to do with it. Sister Mary came over to help me remove the large gold bow, take the red and gold foil paper off the box, and lift the lid. Inside was a teddy bear. I felt sick, as though I were going to faint, but instead I wet my pants. I tried to back away from the table and the bear, but I ended up turning my chair over instead. Everyone was laughing as the nun led me away, and I was certain that this time I was going to be whipped. Instead she took me to my room to change clothes, then sat with me on her lap in the rocking chair, encouraging me to tell her what was wrong. I couldn't.

When she felt that I was calm enough, we walked back to the gym. The teddy bear was still sitting by my place at the table. I froze in the doorway until another nun hid the bear.

Later that night, while everyone was playing with their toys, one of the sisters came to get me and took me to another room where Sister Mary was waiting for me. I sat at the table, wondering what was going to happen. Sister Mary reached under the table and pulled out the bear, sitting it on the table facing me. The other sister sat next to me, rubbing my back and telling me that everything was all right, but I couldn't speak. I could feel my dinner and the party treats rising in my throat. The memories of all the teddy bears, torn and broken at Margie's hands, came flooding back. But I had no words to explain what was wrong.

I didn't want this bear to be destroyed, so I refused to look at it, as though that would prevent the terrible cycle from starting. Both sisters tried to comfort me but it was no use. I vomited on the bear. Once again I had behaved badly, or so I thought, but no one beat me. Instead they cleaned me up and took me back to my room and stayed by me until I fell into a fitful sleep.

A few days later, Pat and Warren came, and they spent a long time talking with the nun in charge while I sat waiting with another of the sisters. And then it was time to go home for Christmas.

Even though I didn't get carsick, I hated the trip to Pat and Warren's house. I wanted to stay at St. Mary's where I was cared for, where people seemed to love me. I was furious that I had been taken away, sure that I would never be going back, and Pat knew it. Soon after arriving at their house the beatings started again, first from Pat and then Warren.

It was too much. All the anger that had been repressed for so long boiled over in a rage. One day while I was home alone, I went up the stairs to my brothers' rooms, knocking over anything in my way. I pulled the books off the shelves and, unaware of my own strength, ripped them to shreds. I pulled the covers off the beds and pushed over lamps before storming into Pat and Warren's room. I took Pat's perfume bottles and smashed them into the full-sized dresser mirror, sending slivers of silvery cut glass falling to the floor. I crawled into their walk-in closet, throwing shoes behind me as I went.

Hearing the noise when they came in, my brothers ran upstairs. When they found me I was flushed and wild-eyed, making unintelligible noises. One of the boys pulled the door closed while another went to get Pat and Warren.

The adults could see that I had almost destroyed the bedrooms, and one grabbed me, pinning me to the floor, while the other went for the belt. The whipping lasted for a long time, and I screamed for the first time since leaving Stoutamyre. Holding me by the hair, Pat dragged me into my bedroom where the whipping continued. When she was finished, the skin on my bottom was as red and broken and bleeding as it had been after one of Margie's beatings. I was sent to bed without dinner.

The next day was Christmas and at Mass I looked everywhere for Sister Mary, hoping she would magically appear and take me away from Pat. I was in so much pain that it was hard to sit. Later that day, when my grandmother came, I was happy because I knew she would protect me. She helped me take a bath and brushed my hair before putting me to bed. Then she lay beside me, carefully avoiding all the sore spots.

Pat didn't like it when Warren's mother came for visits because she couldn't exercise her control over me. One night, unable to sleep, I heard Pat and my grandmother yelling from downstairs. I couldn't understand what they were saying but I felt that it was about me.

When the Christmas holidays were over and it was time to leave, I was ecstatic. If Pat thought she was sending me back to a place like Stoutamyre, she was wrong. St. Mary's was just the opposite, filled with kind and gentle women who encouraged us all.

The nun in charge met our car and welcomed me with her arms as wide as the smile on her face. I ran to her and lost myself in her warm, enveloping hug. I didn't think to wave good-bye to Pat and Warren, going immediately to the playroom to see who else was back. I felt as though I had been away for a long, long time.

After that Christmas visit I reverted to sucking my thumb, and I rocked back and forth when I watched TV. Sometimes the nuns helped us get dressed, and they learned to very carefully avoid the bruises and sores that were reminders of my latest trip home. I limped for a long time after I returned.

In the winter, building snowmen and having snowball fights was permitted. I was afraid, but when Sister Mary herself joined in the fun I relaxed and began to play with the other girls. On nice afternoons the girls often went for bike rides or went roller-skating, and I was anxious to learn too. One of my first attempts ended with me crashing into the wall, raising a knot on my head that I still have.

I continued to excel in school and to earn chips for good behavior. Sometimes I would rebel, throwing and breaking things, but I never laughed or cried. Sister Mary tried everything she knew, from tickling and making faces to putting on clown acts, but I would not laugh. Even when the others laughed at the cartoons on TV, I got scared and moved away. I had learned to fear laughter at Stoutamyre, for I feared the beating that was sure to follow.

Sister Mary encouraged me to talk about my feelings, to tell her what had happened at Stoutamyre and at home, but I was simply too terrified. One day she was crying. The tears were very real but I didn't know that she had cut onions to produce them. She took my hand and touched the teardrops that ran down her cheeks, trying to tell me that it was okay to cry. Her tears made me uncomfortable, and I backed up to get away. I had seen the other girls cry and laugh, but these expressions of emotion still frightened me. It was a good idea, but Sister Mary's onions didn't work either.

I was, however, beginning to learn to relate to the other girls—to play with them, sing and talk with them, and even to hug them. But it was very hard. Just when the ice inside my heart was starting to melt, things changed again.

It was a Saturday. Groups of girls were in the playroom watching movies, relaxing on the comfortable sofas. We had soft drinks and there were bowls of popcorn on the tables. Suddenly a door slammed and we could all hear the sound of angry voices coming from the reception area. The door to the room swung open and there stood Pat, obviously angry and not about to be stopped by the nun grabbing her arm.

Pat spotted me and pulled me to my feet, sending a bowl of popcorn flying. The nun in charge ran to the telephone as Pat pushed me toward the door. Before I could blink we were in the car and Pat was speeding away from the black iron fence.

My heart pounding, my legs like rubber, I huddled near the door as Pat yelled and screamed at the other drivers and at me.

In fear, I wet my pants, but since we had left without my suit-case, I sat in the same clothes, on a plastic bag, the rest of the short drive home.

This time I was home for good. I knew I would never see St. Mary's or Sister Mary again, and my heart was broken. It was the worst feeling. Not a day went by that I didn't think of Sister Mary, and the memory of my last hug comforted me through the nights of renewed pain.

I would have given anything to be with my grandmother. But she had never come to see me at St. Mary's, and I assumed I was so bad that she didn't love me anymore. I never men-tioned her, so the nuns never knew about her. Maybe if they had known about her they would have contacted her and I could have lived with her instead of Warren and Pat.

A few days later a police car pulled into the driveway. War-ren wasn't at home, but Pat invited the two officers in anyway. They talked for a long time in the living room before Pat sent for me to come downstairs. I was very excited, sure that they had come to take me back to Sister Mary. Pat held out her hand as I walked into the room, smiling and hugging me. She sat with her arm around me while she talked. When they left she sent me back upstairs.

I watched from the window as the police car backed out of the driveway. I wanted to pound on the glass and scream for them to come back and get me, but I was afraid. If they didn't hear me, I knew what Pat would do. I watched until the car was out of sight, then locked the door and lay on my bed, looking at the ceiling, lost in memories of St. Mary's. Then I felt some-thing on my face. I touched it and it felt like water. I went to the mirror and saw that I was crying. Sister Mary had taught me that it was okay to cry, so I cried myself to sleep.

6

Warren had been transferred again while I was at St. Mary's. The family was now living in Holliston, Massachusetts. I had only been there for a short time when Pat enrolled me in school. I didn't want another school—I only wanted to go back to St. Mary's. Since we had left in such a rush I needed all new clothes, and Pat decided to use this opportunity to change my appearance. From the very beginning I resented any attempt to make me more like her.

The first appointment was with a beautician. I despised my new hairstyle because it made me look more like Pat, or so I thought, when I really wanted to look like my brothers. They were never beaten or sent to bed without dinner. They had privileges and could go out and play, but I couldn't because I wasn't a boy, whatever that meant. Later we went to try on dresses, and I left looking even more like Pat. My body was beginning to develop curves like Pat's instead of staying flat like my brothers.

One day I was outside playing catch with my brothers. Pat never played catch, so *I* really liked it, until she told the boys that I could no longer play because she wanted me to become a young lady. *A young lady? Now what's that supposed to mean?* Pat tried to explain that football and basketball were for boys. *A boy? A lady? What's the difference? And while we're on the subject, if Pat's a lady, I sure don't want to be one. How can I become a boy like my brothers?* I wondered.

Pat's plan to send me to charm school was a dismal failure. She dropped me off at the door and left to do some shopping of her own. One stylist fixed my hair and another put makeup on my face. One woman tried to teach me how to move in a more feminine way, twisting my hips when I walked. I was sick with fury! Everyone, it seemed, wanted me to look and be like Pat, and I refused. I wiped the makeup off with a towel I found in the bathroom and raked my fingers through my hair to ruin the new style. I went back out and sat, hoping to be left alone until time to go, but no, they kept after me to practice my new walk. I would not be like Pat and that was final! I laid my arm on one end of the counter and swept all the makeup and perfume bottles to the floor then ran into the bathroom to hide.

When I didn't come out to the car at the end of the class, Pat came in to find me and learned of the damage I had done. Barely controlling her anger, she paid for the ruined cosmetics before dragging me to the car. The beatings that evening came as no surprise.

Pat's next attempt to civilize me was ballet class, and she beat me until I put on the tights and leotard. This time she stayed at the class, sitting on the sidelines, to ensure my participation. Pat and Warren never allowed me to wear my hearing aid, insisting that I really didn't have a hearing problem, so following the instructions was difficult. The instructor talked too fast for me to read her speech.

But Pat had brought the hairbrush in her purse. When she believed I wasn't trying, she carefully laid it on her lap as a reminder of what she would do if I didn't dance. At the sight of the hairbrush I renewed my efforts to copy what the other girls were doing.

I tried to persuade my brother to come to the next class with me but he refused, saying that ballet was for girls. There it was again! Ballet was for girls. Pat was a girl. Pat was good at ballet. Therefore, I hated it, for the last thing I wanted to do was follow in her footsteps, either flat-footed or on toe. I was beaten for every class I skipped.

Eventually Pat gave up on ballet and contacted a local Girl Scout troop, where I was again an outcast. The girls didn't understand my speech and laughed at my attempts to talk. Pat tried to force me to associate with the other girls but the more she tried, the more they called me Mommy's girl. I was not a mommy's girl! I didn't have a mommy; I had Pat. Because none of the other girls wanted me in their tent when we went camping, I had to sleep in the tent with Pat, providing her with another excuse and opportunity to whip me.

No amount of charm school or ballet classes was going to provide me with the very basic social skills I lacked. Except for my time at St. Mary's, I had been isolated from normal human contact and had no decent role models for appropriate behavior. My family didn't recognize this as a condition that was forced on me, instead preferring to see it as a symptom of my disability. To make me more acceptable, Pat continued to try to make me over into someone more like her, when all I wanted to do was play sports and dress like my brothers. In my mind, if I dressed like they did and behaved like they did, then I would be treated like they were—with love instead of verbal and physical abuse.

I had two safe places at the house in Holliston: my bedroom and the bathroom with the door locked. From my bedroom I could watch my brothers play, mow the lawn, and rake the grass clippings in the summer and the leaves in the fall. I could watch them wrestle with each other and play basketball. When I thought no one was home I went into my brother's rooms and played with their toys. I wondered why I never had any toys. I took a handful of small plastic soldiers back to my room. One had a mean expression on his army-green face and I named him Pat. Then the rest of the soldiers jumped on him and beat him up. Boy, did that feel good. Knowing I couldn't share these feelings with anyone else, I hid the toys under my bed. My brothers had so many that they never missed them.

One day we had been invited to a neighbor's for dinner and I was supposed to wear a dress. Still wearing my robe, I went to my brother's room to beg for a pair of pants to wear instead. He stood with his back to me, adjusting his tie. *A tie! Now that would be perfect. Pat never wears a tie!* When he refused to give it to me, I grabbed it and tried to pull it off, nearly choking him.

"I want tie on!" I yelled.

"OK, OK, " he gasped, hands clawing at his neck to loosen the slick fabric. He found another tie in his closet and tied it correctly around my neck. I went back to my bedroom, slipped the tie over my head and carefully placed it under my pillow before putting on the dress. The nausea started when Pat came to my room to fix my hair and makeup. When she left to go downstairs I quickly retrieved the tie from under my pillow and slid it over my head, immediately feeling better. Pulling my coat on to cover my secret, I went downstairs to leave with the others.

When we arrived at the neighbors, a man came to take our coats but I refused to take mine off. Pat stepped in front of me, unbuttoned the coat, and saw the tie around my neck. In a flash she unknotted the tie and threw it to the side before taking my hand and pulling me to sit next to her. My brothers went off to play with the children of the household, but Pat didn't want me out of her sight. Later that night I crept into my brother's room to take another tie from his closet. I hid it in my bedroom and tried every spare minute to figure out how to tie the knot.

Another thing that puzzled me was why the toilet seat was always up after one of the boys used the bathroom. Their butts were no bigger than mine, so why did *I* always fall through?

The next time my grandmother came she explained that boys were different—which was not what I wanted to hear—and that they had to raise the seat. She let me know that it was all right to put the seat down when I had to go, instead of holding on to the sides to keep from falling in. No one, least of all Pat, ever explained to me the differences between boys and girls or why my body was changing.

Neither Pat nor Warren sat me down to explain manners, appropriate behavior, or family rules. I had to learn the hard way what to do or not do. Life would have been a lot easier if I knew *why* I couldn't do this or that, or why I was treated differently from my brothers. I began to believe that I was dealing with Margie in a different body. Everyone called her Pat but I knew she was really Margie, only worse. Trying to avoid being beaten by Pat was a full-time job and my goal became to try to get through a day without being hit.

My brothers seemed to know how to live their lives without getting beaten. They knew where to go, what to do, and how to act. How did they learn all these things? Was there an instruction manual that someone had forgotten to give me? I began observing my brothers closely to see what kind of fun I could have without getting punished for it. As soon as Pat would leave to go shopping, my brothers would organize a basketball game and let me play. They would take turns looking out for Pat's return. As soon as she pulled in the driveway the signal went out, and I was rushed inside before she could see me. My game improved and soon I was making baskets. When we played football, my brothers liked that I could throw long passes that made them run. But for the most part, when their friends were around they wanted no part of their strange tomboy sister.

From my brothers I learned how to bait a hook and catch fish in a nearby lake, how to play softball and shoot cans with a BB gun. For a long time I was lucky enough to get back inside before Pat saw me playing with the boys. But one day we really cut it close. They were short one person for their afternoon football game and they asked me to play. I was thrilled, and when one boy caught the ball I tackled him and brought him to the ground like I had seen my brothers do. We were all so caught up in the game that we lost track of time until we saw Pat pulling into the driveway. Pat was moving fast but I was faster as I snuck in the back door and up the stairs to change.

Even though I needed a lot of clothes to replace the ones Pat had left at St. Mary's, I would rather have worn the same thing every day than try on new clothes. Pat was the type of shopper who had to try on every piece of clothing on every rack, so my dressing room had one of everything in it. I got frustrated with the putting on and taking off—on, off, on, off—and accidentally ripped a dress. Then, I thought, if they were all ripped, she wouldn't buy them, so I tore them all and left them in a pile on the floor before putting on my clothes and walking out the door. Pat was in another dressing room and didn't see me leave. *Free at last!* Here was my chance to look for Sister Mary.

A few doors away from the department store was a candy store. I was hungry, and the sight of the Hershey bars made me even more homesick for Sister Mary, so I picked one up, unwrapped it, and bit into the sweet milk chocolate. Back on the street I continued my search for women wearing the black robes of St. Mary's. I had forgotten all about Pat, but she hadn't forgotten me. After leaving another store with another candy bar, I saw her pull up to the curb and jump from the car. As she pushed me into the front seat I saw the bags of clothes in the back. Pat had no difficulty driving and slapping me at the same time. When we arrived home, she finished the whipping and stood with hairbrush in hand while I tried on all the clothes. They were all too tight.

Pat made me vacuum and clean the house. One day I asked Peter why the boys never had to clean and he said it was because I was a lady. There was that word again. Finally I sat him down and asked him what a lady was and how I was supposed to be one.

"Don't worry about it, Anne," he said. "You were a mistake. You were really supposed to be a boy. Daddy wanted all boys, no girls."

I was a mistake? How could that be?

"Then where did I come from?" I asked.

"You came from a stork. The storks take the babies to the hospital and the parents pick them up there," he explained. "When Daddy went to the hospital to bring home the new baby, he picked you up by mistake. He was supposed to bring home another boy. You're someone else's baby." And with that, he left the room.

Of course, I believed him. If it weren't true, why would he have said it? I sat on the sofa in shock, feeling a sharp pain in my chest, even though no one had hit me there. All I could think was that I didn't belong there.

On another occasion, while trying to learn to play my brother Peter's trumpet, I accidentally woke Pat. I marched around the house as I blew, just like I'd seen my brothers doing, not realizing how loud the sound was. Pat roared out of her bedroom and grabbed the trumpet and began chasing me with it. I ran down the stairs and she followed me, tripping on the carpet as she entered the living room. Warren sent me to my room as he helped her back upstairs.

One brother came in and took the trumpet away. "Why are you always causing trouble?" he shouted.

Trouble? How was I causing trouble? I only wanted to learn how to play the trumpet like they did.

"All you're life you've been trouble. Dad told us you're the reason Mom died. Why don't you go back to where you were before?" he asked.

Mom died? What was that all about? I thought Pat was Mom, and she was very much alive. I went to my room and thought about what my brothers had said. Even though none of it made any sense, I believed everything they said. Someone called Mom had died because of me, and I didn't belong there. That's why I was treated differently from them. They got something they called love that I never got. What was it? Where did you get it and how much did it cost? *Maybe,* I thought, *my life would be easier if I had some of this love. But then, maybe not.* All I wanted was a life with no beatings.

I hated holidays. At Christmas my brothers got toys, cameras, watches, art kits, puzzles, and baseball mitts. I got jewelry boxes, earrings, and necklaces, but no toys. What was I going to do with all that stuff?

At Easter Pat always bought me dresses with lace and flowers and ruffles. I had to wear stiff patent leather shoes with buckles that hurt, crinkly slips under the dress, and some kind of bow in my hair. And I had to sit like a statue so I didn't mess anything up. My brothers always looked so comfortable in their dress pants, comfortable shoes, and sports jackets.

I never knew what was going on in church or why we were there. Even at St. Mary's, I just followed what everybody else did. Pat's church, though, was a lot different than St. Mary's, where the only women were nuns wearing habits. But here, all the females were dressed like Pat. They all looked alike, dressed alike, wore makeup and lipstick, carried purses, and wore fancy hats. So there was more than one Pat in the world!

Once we went to New Jersey to visit my grandmother. The entire time we were there I was never out of her sight. She hugged me constantly and told me how much she loved me. At bedtime she sat beside me, reading me stories or just talking to me. Even though I didn't understand everything she said, she made me feel special just by spending time with me. How I wanted to be special!

The night before we were to leave I snuck into my grandmother's room and woke her up. Everyone else was sleeping but she closed the door anyway and turned on the light. I sat on her bed and told her everything. I told her about Stoutamyre and about every beating since I'd been home from St. Mary's. I told her that I didn't want to go back to Holliston with Pat, that I wanted to stay and live with her. With tears in her eyes, she hugged me and sent me back to bed, promising to talk to my father the next morning. I fell into a deep and dreamless sleep.

I woke up before my brothers, but the grown-ups were already up. As I tiptoed down the stairs, even I could hear Warren and Pat's voices, though not their words. Their yelling woke up one of my brothers, who joined me at the foot of the stairs. He began to whisper what they were saying so I could read his lips. My grandmother was asking them if I could come to live with her. Pat said that under no circumstances would that happen. My brother listened closely, trying to repeat exactly what they were saying.

"Don't you think you did enough damage to that innocent little girl by sending her to that cruel place?" my grandmother asked. "I've seen how you abuse her. And you call that love?"

Taking her words literally, I thought she meant beating was love. I suddenly didn't want any love.

Eventually everyone was up and the tension was thick. Red-faced and angry, Pat made no pretense of patience and ordered everyone around. "Brush your teeth! Comb your hair! Pick up your shoes! Get into the car!" Each command was shouted. No one was spared, not even Warren.

The connection between my grandmother and me was a tangible thing as I clung to her. When it was time to go, Pat squeezed my arm as she pulled me away. As we drove off I watched my grandmother growing smaller and smaller, a tissue held to her face, as Pat ordered Warren, "Hurry up and get out of here."

Pat had made me sit up front with her, and now she began brushing my hair hard, telling me that I was always starting trouble and that she didn't want me to have any contact with my grandmother again. She ended the conversation with a whack across my head with the hairbrush. Later, when I looked in the rear view mirror I saw a large red mark on the side of my face.

After that visit Pat and Warren had a lot of arguments about my grandmother. She never came to visit again as long as Pat lived with us.

That August, Peter and I celebrated our birthday. I think we were either twelve or thirteen. A few days later, I went to public school. Wearing a dress, I followed Pat into the principal's office. After a brief meeting, during which I could hear nothing because I hadn't been allowed to wear my hearing aid, I was taken to the special education class. The principal introduced me to the teacher and the ten other students, but I refused to say a word. I didn't want a new teacher, I wanted Sister Mary!

After getting the other students started on their lesson, the teacher took me to a small table at the rear of the room. I sat down and looked warily around the room. The teacher gave me a book to read out loud, but there were no pictures on the page. The books at St. Mary's all had pictures. How was I supposed to know what the words said without pictures? I closed the book.

Then the teacher gave me some math problems. I had learned to do addition and subtraction but some of these problems had an $\times$ and some had a $\overline{)}$, a symbol that I had never seen before. I added the ones with the $\times$, thinking that the $+$

symbol had just gotten tilted. The ones with the $\overline{)}$ symbol, I ignored. After the math exercise the teacher gave me a piece of paper and a pencil and motioned for me to write something. At St. Mary's I had a sheet with the alphabet on it to copy from, and without it I couldn't even write my own name.

Later that afternoon, alone in my bedroom, I took off the dress and stared in the mirror at my changing body. My chest was developing like Pat's, and I now had to wear a white strap-thing that hooked in the back. I slipped on my robe and went into my brother's room. I rummaged through his dresser draw-ers until I found what I was looking for—a large T-shirt and a pair of blue jeans. I felt much better. I went back to my room, took all the dresses out of the closet, and carried them to my brother's room where I hung them out of sight in the back of his closet.

I stood in front of the mirror again. The image was chang-ing but there was still something that needed to be done. My brothers all had short hair but mine was long—like Pat's. I went downstairs to the desk, found a pair of scissors, took them with me to the bathroom, and locked the door behind me. When I was finished, my hair was short all around—not very even, but I didn't think anyone would notice. I went back to my room and checked out my reflection in the mirror one more time. This time I was pleased, because I looked more like my brothers. Surely now I wouldn't get beaten.

When it was time for dinner, I tucked the T-shirt into the waistband of the blue jeans, brushed my new short hair, and walked downstairs. Everyone was talking as I walked into the dining room but the conversation quickly ceased as first one brother, then another, turned to look at me. They acted as though they had never seen me before. I could tell from the expression on Pat's face that I had been wrong about the beat-ings. Looking like my brothers was not the answer.

After a few weeks at school, one by one the teachers called for a meeting with Warren and Pat, saying that I couldn't follow along in class. Warren told them that I loved the attention that I got by pretending to be deaf. After Warren's visit, when I asked to have something repeated, the teacher told me to stop playing and pay attention. I spent many nights crying myself to sleep in frustration.

Not long after this, as part of a routine vision and hearing screening, the school nurse referred me to a hearing specialist. Furious at me for creating a scene (as they called it), Pat and Warren threatened to take me back to Stoutamyre if I didn't stop pretending that I couldn't hear. For a very long time I believed them when they said it was all in my head.

After the first day of school I rode the bus every day and walked to and from the bus stop alone. My brothers feared rejection from their friends if they walked with me. Lunchtime at school was not pleasant. Because we never had enough lunch money to go around, I brought lunch in a brown paper sack from home, usually a peanut-butter-and-jelly or bologna sandwich. Since the other students made fun of the way I sat, walked, and talked, I usually ate lunch in the bathroom. Since leaving St. Mary's I had reverted to many of my behaviors from Stoutamyre, including rocking.

One day I hid behind the house when the bus came and walked to a nearby store instead. Not knowing I should pay for it, I took a handful of candy and gum and put it in my lunch bag. I had no concept of money or what it was for. I wandered around for a while until I got bored and then walked to school where I started passing out the candy. As long as I had sweets everyone liked me—I had friends. Soon I was surrounded by a group of students at lunch, and I made up stories about my life. I wanted so badly for them to think of me as normal and accept me. The other students were happy when I lied about my age because it meant I could buy cigarettes for them. Every day someone gave me a piece of green paper and told me to give it to the shopkeeper in exchange for their favorite brand. For the first time I was popular. I told Peter so he could see that I was just like him.

My false popularity was short-lived, however. On chilly days I had been wearing one of my brother's jackets, which had many pockets. I filled each of the pockets with as many different kinds of candy as I could. The storeowner stopped me as I was walking out and made me empty all my pockets out on the counter. He told me that I was to pay for all the candy. *Pay? What did that word mean?* Somehow he must have known my telephone number, because soon Pat walked in. I heard the word "stealing" but didn't understand. I thought stealing meant taking something from another person, not from a store. After paying the storeowner, she grabbed me by the ear and drove me home.

Up in my room, Pat told me to take off all my clothes. My body was still covered with bruises from the last beating and I didn't want any more pain. I tried to get away but tripped and she was on top of me with the hairbrush before I could rise. Unsatisfied with the brush, she got up to get the belt but I moved faster and escaped to the bathroom, locking the door before collapsing on the floor gasping for breath. As Pat pounded on the door I slowly rose to my feet and looked in the mirror. My lip was split and swollen from the hairbrush, and my arms were red and painful. I leaned against the wall and slid to the floor again. *What,* I wondered, *can I do to be treated like my brothers? What am I doing wrong?*

After the knocking had stopped for a long time, I turned the lock and peeked into the hallway. No one was there. I covered myself with a towel and tiptoed down to my room, locked the door, and turned around to see Pat standing in the closet, holding a black-and-white-checked dinner dress on a hanger. Standing with the hairbrush in her hand, she waited while I put on the low-cut dress. Bobby socks and loafers completed the outfit she had selected. Then she took me to her dressing table where she combed my hair and applied heavy makeup to my face to cover the bruises. Then she drove me to school.

Perspiring heavily, I walked in the classroom and tried to take my seat without attracting any attention, but it was no use. Everyone turned and stared, and as the sweat poured off my face, the makeup went with it, revealing the bruises and swelling underneath.

The teacher took me to the principal's office, but when I was too afraid to answer his questions he called Pat. She walked in, appearing to be full of concern, and asked me what had happened. Before I could answer she stepped hard on my toes as a warning. I don't know what she told him as an explanation for the bruises, but apparently it was convincing. When she asked if I could go home to rest, I hoped the principal would say no, but he told me to go home with my mother.

As soon as we were in the car and off the school property, Pat found the hairbrush in her purse and began to beat my face again. Pat was never one to let the sight of existing bruises slow her down, and she continued the beating after we arrived home. Rather than attempt to hide the new bruises, she kept me out of school for the rest of the term.

No one noticed me unless I did something wrong. I didn't know how to behave around other people to avoid being beaten, so I began spending more and more time alone in my room. It was lonely, but safer. I often cried myself to sleep, holding my pillow and wishing it were Sister Mary. I looked for her face in every crowd of people. When Pat wasn't around I would slip into my baby brother Bill's room and rock myself to sleep in the rocking chair, sucking my thumb.

By far the cruelest thing anyone ever did to me wasn't the beatings or the starving or being tied to a chair—it was being given someone to love, who loved me, and then having that person removed from my life forever. I would never have learned to feel what was in my heart if I hadn't known Sister Mary, but it made life with my family so much harder. I was told that this was *my* family. *Family? What was that?* I was told that a family consisted of a mother, father, and brothers who loved me.

It was a confusing concept, but I had finally accepted what "love" meant: pain. No love, no pain. Pat said that Margie loved me. Pat said that *she* loved me, and yet both women caused me pain. My brothers never told me they loved me and they never physically hurt me. Love, therefore, surely meant pain. I kept that philosophy for a very long time. Then when I was no longer being beaten, I accepted the fact that no one loved me.

Things are tough enough when you're a teenager, but being rejected by your own family makes it worse. I was never included when Warren and my brothers played Monopoly or other board games. They all believed that I was too retarded to understand how to play. When they had their friends over I was supposed to stay in my room so their friends wouldn't see me. I know now that this is not uncommon between brothers and sisters in healthy families, but in ours it was complicated by my many differences. My brothers were clearly ashamed of me. I followed one of my brothers once when he went on his paper route, and when he saw me, he made me walk on the other side of the street. When one of his friends approached and asked who I was, he said that he didn't know *what* I was. *What* I was, not *who* I was. When I stole my brothers' paper route money and piggy banks they began showing signs of not only being ashamed but also genuinely not liking me.

I had begun developing a great curiosity about mechanical things, so one day when Peter left the riding lawn mower idling in the yard while he ran inside, I went over to look at it. Even though my brothers had always done the mowing, I could visualize myself sitting on the machine. The realization that I had never seen Pat on the lawnmower added fuel to my desire to mow the lawn. I climbed on the rumbling machine and held my breath. *Now, to figure out how to get it to move.* I saw a lever with a black knob on the end and pulled it down. Success! The mower jerked forward. I wasn't holding on to the wheel and was thrown off, but the mower kept moving. The fence stopped the mower and a rock stopped my head. My brother ran across the yard, waving his arms and yelling.

Later that night, when dessert was served, I screamed with my first spoonful of ice cream and grabbed my mouth in pain. Pat discovered a tooth that had been broken in half. My brother told her about the lawn mower incident and my fall. Pat was furious that I had been so foolish and she dragged me from the table into the bathroom. My brothers were angry with me, saying that now we couldn't go on vacation. For a long time, I didn't connect the cost for a new cap on my front tooth and the lack of money for vacation.

One brilliantly sunny summer day my brothers were all gone, either to Boy Scout meetings, paper routes, or playing with friends. Pat was lying in the backyard in the sun. I walked through the house and down the basement stairs to get my brother's BB gun. I had seen my younger brothers play cowboys and Indians and had watched westerns on TV. I took the BB gun outside and pedaled away on my bicycle, whooping and yelling like the cowboys did in the movies.

When I stopped the bike and turned around, I saw Pat sleeping on her back in the lawn chair. I hid in some bushes and slowly aimed the gun, visualizing the BBs entering her skin and causing her to yell out in pain. And then I was laughing! I could laugh! I laughed so hard that tears rolled down my cheeks. But the laughter didn't diffuse the anger that welled up inside me, and I began laughing and crying at the same time.

Through the tears of frustration and rage and bone-deep loneliness, I raised the gun again, located Pat in the sight, and pulled the trigger. BANG! I had shot her! I couldn't tell where the BB hit, but she got up fast. She couldn't see me in my hiding place so I aimed again and fired a few more times, hitting her at least once more before she could make it to the house, holding her leg as she went. Adrenaline surged through my body and I felt powerful! I had given her pain; not as much as she had given me, but still pain. It was a good feeling.

By the time I came back from hiding the gun under a neighbor's flowering shrub, the adrenaline was beginning to wear off, leaving a numbing fear in its place. I stayed outside for a long time, afraid to go in. I knew what I had done was horribly wrong, and I also knew what would happen if anyone found out that I had done it.

When I finally worked up the courage to go inside, Pat was in bed. She stayed there through dinner and the rest of the night. Good, I thought. It will keep her away from me. The following morning Warren came to talk with all of us during breakfast. He asked each of us where we had been the previous afternoon when Pat had been shot with the BB gun. All of my brothers had been miles from home. All eyes were on me when I said that I had been riding my bike in the neighborhood. My face was on fire as I lied and said that I hadn't done it. Warren wanted to know how the BB gun had gotten from the basement to the neighbor's yard. I knew I was in trouble but still played dumb and acted as though I had no idea what had happened.

Warren told me to stay at the table while my brothers cleared the dishes away. I hated the silent treatment because it meant that I was really going to get it this time. The longer I had to wait, the more nervous I became. My heart was racing and my body was drenched with sweat as I looked to my brothers for some kind of support or sympathy. I got nothing. I was both frustrated and scared at the same time—frustrated because I had been trying to release some of my pent-up anger but the anger was still there, and scared because I knew what was coming.

Why don't they just whip me and get it over with instead of making me sit here and wait for so long? I wondered. It never occurred to me that the anxiety caused by waiting was a part of the punishment. Sitting at the table, imagining the beating to come, I became so upset that I wet my pants.

Finally my brothers were finished in the kitchen and they went outside without even a glance at me. Warren came in carrying a wide belt. This was it. Warren walked slowly over to me and took my hand, leading me to the basement stairs. My legs felt like they were made of rubber bands, and I had trouble walking down the stairs. In the basement, Warren had me pull my pants down and bend over a table while he whipped me with the belt for so long that I lost track of time. When Warren left, my body was vibrating with pain. As I started to pull my wet pants up, the basement door opened once more and Pat limped down the stairs.

Pat didn't use a belt or a hairbrush this time; she used her fists. She pounded, kicked, and punched me all over. She screamed at me, telling me how much she hated me and wished I were dead. She picked up a book and threw it at me, yelling all the while. She raved about how much she despised me, saying she should have let me stay where I belonged. Where *did* I belong? Her anger fueled itself, and the more she hit, the angrier she got. Finally she cornered me and began slapping the side of my head. One of the blows slammed my head into the stone wall of the basement and everything went black as I slid down the wall to the floor.

When I awoke the next day, I still lay where I'd fallen. I couldn't unfold my legs or straighten up at the waist. Even short, shallow breaths made my chest ache. I felt the side of my head and found my hair sticky with blood. My eyes were swollen almost shut, and my fingers felt like thick sausages. My lips were bulging, and swallowing caused terrible pain.

As I lay there, unable to move any part of my body without pain, I thought of Sister Mary. If Pat truly hated me as much as she said, why had she taken me away from St. Mary's? If she had left me there, she would never have had to see me. It made no sense. Then I remembered how good I felt after I had shot her with the BB gun. Maybe beating me up all the time made Pat feel good.

No one came to check on me, but I later found enough energy to walk a little. My stomach was so sore from her punches that I couldn't straighten up. I thought of going up to my room and going to bed. Breathing was difficult and every part of me was stiff as I tried climbing the basement stairs. I don't know how long it took, but when I finally reached the top, the door was locked. Not wanting to attract any attention, I didn't dare pound on the door; I wouldn't have had the strength to do it anyway. Out of breath and out of energy, I painfully inched my way back down. I lay down at the bottom of the stairs, knees drawn up, curled around my pain.

More time passed, maybe as much as a day. I slept much of the time, finding one semi-pain-free position and not moving. When awake, I relived my time at St. Mary's. I had chosen to sleep facing the basement door, as I had done in the room with no lights and no windows at Stoutamyre.

When the door finally opened, fear and pain coursed through my body. Pat was smiling as she walked toward me. I feared the worst. She reached down to help me up, but I couldn't straighten my body. After an agonizing trip up the stairs to my bedroom, she had me take off my stiff, urine- and blood-caked clothes.

Uh-oh! Here it comes—another whipping! Will she never get enough?

But after helping me put on my robe, she took me to the bathroom where the tub was filling with water. I realized with horror that she was planning to give me a bath. I knew I couldn't get into the water. Sick and dizzy with pain, I turned to look in the mirror—my face was unrecognizable even to me.

As it turned out, Pat decided to give me a sponge bath, but every touch with the warm, wet washcloth brought a scream of pain that I couldn't stifle. Dizzy and lightheaded, I sank to the cool tile floor. Pat lifted my head. She held a glass of prune juice to my lips and handed me three long pills. She helped me stand and took me back to my bed, pulling back the covers and lowering my head to the pillow. Even the weight of the sheets hurt, but the pills I had taken eventually made me sleep.

When I woke up, Pat was sitting beside the bed. She left for a few minutes and when she returned, she was carrying a tray with a bowl of chicken soup, some crackers, a pitcher of ice water, and a glass with a long straw that bent in the middle. She began feeding me the soup a spoonful at a time and broke crackers into tiny pieces and put them between my swollen, cracked, and blood-caked lips. Swallowing was agony, but she was patient and sat until I had eaten most of the soup. Then she picked up the glass and held the straw to my mouth. No matter how I tried, my lips wouldn't fit completely around the straw and water dribbled down my chin and onto the sheet. But, amazingly, Pat didn't get mad. Instead, she gently blotted my chin with a napkin. When I woke from the next nap I was shocked to see a small TV set on the dresser at the foot of the bed.

After each feeding, Pat gave me more pills and, as I lay in the bed watching TV, sleep overtook me again. Somehow Pat managed to keep my brothers and Warren out of the room until my visible wounds were nearly healed.

I must have been in my room for a week or more and my energy was slowly returning, but I was afraid to leave. I didn't know why Pat had decided to be so nice to me, but I wasn't about to let my guard down in case she changed her mind.

7

When I was in my late teens, we went to New Jersey for a short vacation. I was introduced to aunts, uncles, and cousins on my father's side of the family. My aunt had photo albums of all of us as tiny children. She showed me pictures of my grandmother holding me and Peter and another photo of a woman holding just me. When I asked who the woman was, she said, "Why, honey, that's your real mommy."

Peter then explained that Pat was not our real mom. I was confused. *How could someone have more than one mom?* I asked where this real mommy was. Peter said she was dead.

Then they showed me another picture of the same woman, this time in a wedding dress standing next to my father. The next picture was of Warren and Pat when they were married. We got in the car and drove a short distance to the cemetery and walked to my mother's grave. As I stood looking at the gravestone with her name on it, the world around me dissolved, leaving only the grave. I squatted down to touch the marker and ran my fingers slowly over her name, tracing the outline of each letter.

I kept staring at the ground and asking myself, *Why?* Why had my mother left me like this? Could it be that she hadn't loved me? Maybe it *was* really my fault. Then Peter walked up to me and said, "Now you know why Pat is so mean to us. It's because she's not our mother."

I was surprised to find out my brothers had been mistreated, too; I had never seen them punished.

I tried to understand the concept of a mother other than Pat, but couldn't. *This must be a joke,* I thought. My brothers loved to say crazy things and make me believe them. If this were true, I would have known about it before now. Surely my grandmother would have told me. She never joked or played around. She would have told me Pat wasn't my real mother. Deep inside though, I knew it was true and my hatred of Pat intensified.

The next time I saw my grandmother, I wasted no time asking, "Is my real mother dead?" My grandmother was surprised and at a loss for words. I suddenly remembered another visit, finding a picture in her dresser drawer of a young woman. At the time she wouldn't tell me who the woman was and scolded me for snooping in her room. I had forgotten about finding that picture until now. While my grandmother was searching for the words to answer my question, I ran to her room and found the picture again. When I returned to the living room, I walked over to my grandmother and handed her the picture, asking if this woman was my real mother.

My grandmother stared at the picture for a long while. Her face was white, like she'd seen a ghost. Then, seeing my impatience, she said in a low voice, "Yes, Anne, this is Joan, and she's your real mother."

I was furious that everyone, even the two youngest boys, had known—everyone but me. My grandmother said that she had been ordered by my father and Pat never to tell me. Now that someone else had told me first, she was freed from her promise not to tell and relieved to be able to talk to me about my mother. She knew I had a right to know.

When I asked why I was sent away to Stoutamyre, she sat me down and told me the story.

The woman in the photos was my birthmother, Joan. She and her two brothers had grown up in Schenectady, New York in the 1930s. Being the only female in her class at MIT had not been easy, but Joan graduated with high honors, earning her degree in architectural engineering. She met my father Warren at a social gathering a few years after World War II ended.

Warren was an only child. My grandmother was very intelligent and encouraged him to make education a high priority. Like my mother, he majored in engineering and graduated with high honors from a university in New York. As soon as he was hired at his first job—even before he married my mother—Warren set up a trust fund for his future children's college education.

Soon after their marriage, Joan and Warren started their family. Mark came first, then two years later Dan was born. Joan was often ill during the year after Dan's birth and didn't regain her energy as quickly as she had following her first delivery. After several doctors' visits and many different tests, Joan was diagnosed with cancer. Soon after the diagnosis, their third son, Paul, was born.

Joan's doctor warned that another pregnancy would speed the spread of cancer and advised her not to have any more children. Joan was bedridden for a long time, and then she announced in late 1953 that she was pregnant again. As her doctor predicted, the cancer began to spread throughout Joan's body. While she was pregnant with my brother and me, she had surgery to amputate one leg. Years later my grandmother told me that the doctors speculated that the morphine my mother had been given for pain had affected my hearing. After a very difficult delivery, I was able to go home but both my mother and Peter, my twin brother, had to stay in the hospital.

Warren alternated his time between work and visiting his wife and new young son in the hospital. Even after Joan came home, she wasn't well. She slept almost constantly as her damaged immune system fought to rid her body of simple infections. At some point the family moved to Roanoke, Virginia, leaving Peter and me with our grandparents so that Joan could have time to recover.

Joan died in Roanoke, from complications following a cold, almost three years after Peter's and my birth. During her long battle with cancer she remained strong-willed and amazingly cheerful. She was never without a smile for family and friends alike. Her funeral was large and attended by not only friends and family, but also neighbors, college classmates, fellow church members, and others from the community.

Pat, one of Warren's secretaries, had been very supportive when Joan was ill and it wasn't long before she and my father fell in love and got married. It had been Warren's idea to marry quickly for the children's sake but it wasn't so easy for his new bride to inherit a ready-made family. Nevertheless, Pat soon released the nanny Warren had hired and began caring for Mark, Dan, and Paul.

Peter and I remained in New Jersey with our grandparents. My grandmother told me that my behavior caused problems, and that she and my grandfather had a difficult time disciplining me. I didn't react when my name was called or pay attention when people spoke to me. At nursery school, I wandered around the classroom and didn't respond when the teacher called me to sit down. One day I went outside to go on the slide when no one else was around. I climbed up the slide instead of the ladder, slipped, and fell to the ground, breaking my leg. The teacher's helper, who had followed me outside, found me on the ground in pain and in tears.

My twin brother Peter and I had lived with our grandparents for about three-and-a-half years when the adults decided that Peter was ready to live at home with his other brothers and to get to know his new mother. I was supposed to go home when Pat felt ready to accept the challenge of parenting me.

Yet my grandmother began losing patience. She couldn't understand why I wouldn't obey. She tried in vain to get me to repeat the words she said: *Grandma, Daddy, apple, cat.* She was frustrated by her son, who seemed to have forgotten that he had a daughter. Finally she called Warren to remind him that his daughter needed to be with the rest of her family. Perhaps I missed Peter, she reasoned; he and I had gotten along well the little time we had spent together. It was a little more than a year after Peter left when my father, convinced of his responsibilities at last, brought me home.

Pat and Warren had no better luck than my grandparents had. I wouldn't sit still and didn't listen when they talked to me. Pat's Southern upbringing and emphasis on etiquette were wasted on her new stepdaughter. Even though Peter and I were the same age, I didn't know how to talk like he did. When I wanted something, I pointed to it or took someone by the hand to show them. Pat, like my grandmother, began losing patience. Between work during the day and meetings in the evening, Warren was hardly ever home and Pat didn't know what to do with me.

Although I don't remember it, Pat apparently brought me to Johns Hopkins Hospital and asked them to test and see if I was retarded. I first went in October, 1959 when I was five years old. The earliest records (which I found many years later) stated that I had "mental and developmental retardation," and had difficulty hearing speech. A doctor noted on one of my charts that "Anne appeared to enjoy and profit by periods of being observed and talked to. It would seem wise for her to have as much opportunity to have language and speech stimulation with one or two people in a quiet situation as can possibly be worked out. It is difficult for the untrained observer to note that she actually can do many things, despite some of her obvious difficulties." For Pat, the logical solution was to send me away. My father resisted at first but eventually gave in to his wife's wishes.

Pat's father knew a woman who operated a special school for children with mental and physical disabilities. Pat argued that I would get better care if I lived with people who were trained to take care of my special needs.

My grandmother said that when she found out I had been sent to Stoutamyre, she was very angry and called my father begging him to let me live with her again. Warren and Pat refused. Finally my grandparents found out where I was and came to visit me, much to Margie's shock. She hadn't known about my grandmother and felt cornered when she suddenly appeared. Margie allowed my grandparents to see me, but soon after she called Pat and Warren.

Pat was furious when Margie told her my grandparents had come to visit. She told Warren that she didn't want my grandmother interfering in their lives. Pat's obsession for control had led to Warren turning all authority over to her, including the decision about where I would live. She said my grandmother could still came to visit, but not very often.

When I ran away after the trip to the World's Fair, Margie told Pat and Warren that my grandparents were too disruptive an influence and recommended that they be kept away entirely. Pat, of course, agreed with Margie and told her that I was to have no visitors except her and Warren. When my grandmother showed up at Stoutamyre, Margie was to turn her away. Margie was only too happy to oblige.

Then it was my grandmother's turn to threaten. She contacted an attorney to sue for custody. She suspected I was being mistreated at Stoutamyre, but she didn't have any details. Pat swore that she would send me to a place where my grandparents could never find me if they continued with the lawsuit, but agreed to allow them to visit if my grandmother withdrew the suit. Rather than lose all contact with me, my grandmother dismissed the attorney. My grandmother was forced to limit her visits, but she continued to occasionally take me away for weekends.

When my grandmother did see me, she was concerned by what she saw. I wasn't the same little girl she had raised. She was deeply hurt by the changes in me, but her hands were tied. She took great care to show me love and affection when I visited her, but most of the time I didn't respond.

When I was sent to St. Mary's, Pat made sure my grandmother never found out where I was, which explained why she had never visited me. My grandmother told me she had cried on my birthday because she couldn't send me a card or gift or even call.

I remembered well the Christmas I came home from St. Mary's. My grandmother had been so happy to see me, but was shocked to see the marks on my body. She begged to be allowed to take me home with her—but again Pat refused. That was the argument I had heard. Pat hated having my grandmother around. She couldn't whip me or send me to bed without supper when my grandmother was there.

I was overwhelmed by what my grandmother told me that day. It explained so much: why the only grandparents I knew had been on my father's side of the family, why my brothers resented me, why I had never known the love of a mother. Finally, I understood why Pat hated me—I looked like my mother, the first woman my father had loved. I redoubled my efforts to fit in and to make my father proud of me.

8

Warren was transferred to Cleveland the summer when I was about fourteen, and Peter and I made the move with him. Pat came later with the two youngest boys, Rick and Bill. My oldest brother was in Vietnam and Dan rarely came home from college. Paul, though, came home over winter and summer breaks from college.

Because of my late start in the public school system and the time I had missed, I was in the ninth grade again. This time I had a special counselor who made sure I was placed in the right math, English, and writing classes. Her name was Miss Nancy and she reminded me a lot of Sister Mary. My schedule was arranged so I could see Miss Nancy often during the day. Before class she checked to make sure I had my homework, pencils, and papers, and afterwards we went over how the class had gone. I often spent my free hour or lunchtime in her office while she took care of paperwork. She was sure to have a candy bar and a soda waiting. I began working hard in school, trying to stay out of trouble, so I could continue to see Miss Nancy.

It must have been painfully obvious to her that I wasn't adjusting well. I had difficulty paying attention in class and had no study skills. Miss Nancy was patient with me and spoke with the teachers on my behalf. This only served to confuse the teachers who were repeatedly told by Warren and Pat that I would do anything to get attention, including pretending to be deaf.

One day Miss Nancy met with Pat and Warren and asked if she could take me out to dinner. Much to my surprise, they gave their permission. Pat picked out my clothes and although I hated them, I would have worn anything just to be able to go.

After the meal Miss Nancy had me read out loud to her for a while and then she began asking me questions about my family, how many brothers I had, and so forth. The reading had gone well but now my tongue froze to the roof of my mouth and I couldn't speak. I stared at her, unable to talk about my family, hoping she wouldn't hit me for not answering. She wasn't angry that I didn't answer her questions—perhaps my lack of answers said more than my words could have—and later we went to a movie.

After that evening, Miss Nancy often invited me to her home. She wanted to help me close the gap between my peers and me, and arranged for me to attend summer school the following year.

Unable or unwilling to adjust to life in the Midwest, Pat moved back East after a short time and took Bill and Rick with her. I was so happy! No more beatings! The most Warren ever did was yell at us. My brothers were happy too, and finally told me of beatings they had received at Pat's hands as well. They said they hadn't been aware of many of my beatings either. Pat, like Margie, was a master at concealing her cruelty.

Warren was traveling a lot for work and needed help taking care of the house and Peter and me. He asked my grandmother to come live with us and, anxious to make up for all the missed years, she sold her house in New Jersey to my cousin and joined us in Ohio.

When Warren wasn't on the road with his job, he spent a lot of time with my brother, helping with his homework and playing games. We had weekly family meetings but everyone talked too fast for me to follow their conversations. Whenever I asked someone to repeat what was said, the answer was always, "Later." When later came, the answer was, "Never mind, it wasn't important."

One rare day Warren sat me down for a conversation. "Now that Pat's gone, I expect you to be on your best behavior," he said sternly. "Do your best in school and don't do anything to cause trouble or I'll send you back to Stoutamyre." I knew he would do it, too. It was a full-time job not to make any mistakes. If I wasn't sure whether to do something, I wouldn't do it. It was safer than paying for it later.

Having so much free time was as stressful as his threat. My life at Stoutamyre had been completely regimented and Pat had organized my days since St. Mary's. Now I had to determine when to get up, when to go to bed, and what to do on weekends. My brothers were always busy with their friends and didn't want me around. My grandmother was busy with the housework and didn't want my help. I had more time to be with friends, but I didn't have any.

Our house had a swimming pool, and Peter and Paul often invited their friends over for swimming parties. I thought if I invited some of the girls from school over then maybe I would begin to have some friends. But the girls I invited were more interested in flirting with Peter. One day as I came out with the snacks my grandmother had prepared, I saw one of the girls say, "I can't believe she's so dumb! Maybe she's retarded or something."

"But who cares?" the other one said. "At least she's got this pool, and a cute brother, too."

I went back inside and stayed in my room the rest of the afternoon. It was the last time I invited anyone over to swim.

When I began passing out in school I was taken to the hospital for tests. I was diagnosed with epilepsy and was given medicine to control the seizures. The doctor said that a possible cause was blows to the head and that it looked as though, in the past, I had been repeatedly struck with something.

Despite the confirmation by medical professionals, Warren tried to make me believe that I was faking again, this time faking "spells," as he called them, to get attention. My grandmother believed her son and had agreed when she moved in with us that she wouldn't interfere with how Warren raised us. He made me stop taking the medicine.

It wasn't long before the seizures returned, and the doctor learned through blood tests that I didn't have the drug in my system. When the doctor patiently explained to me the importance of taking the medication, I told him that my father told me to stop taking it. My father then pulled the doctor aside and talked fast and softly, his back to me. I later found out that he told the doctors that he tried and tried to get me to take my medicine but I refused.

After this pattern repeated itself several times, I quit going to the doctor and did everything possible to keep people from seeing me have a seizure at school. If I thought one was coming on, I hid in the bathroom and splashed cold water on my face. It worked sometimes, but not always. Every time someone saw me pass out at school Warren punished me for it. He yelled at me, threatening to whip me, and made me stay in my room.

Before the end of the school year, Warren was transferred again, this time to Ann Arbor, Michigan. I would have to start over in a new school without Miss Nancy.

I fell into my old pattern of watching my brothers and copying them in order to appear more normal. I acted like they did, ate the way they ate, walked the way they walked. When they flirted with girls, I flirted with girls, not knowing that this wasn't socially acceptable. I thought it was fun and liked it when the others laughed, not realizing that they were laughing *at* me, not *with* me.

When my grandmother saw that I was flirting with girls and acting like "one of the boys," she stepped in. She bought me dresses and more feminine clothes, but I threw them in the fireplace. I vowed that my grandmother wasn't going to make me over into another Pat. The more she tried, the more I rebelled. She was upset that we were no longer close. She felt that Pat had ruined me and destroyed the relationship we once had. I was stubborn and refused to become a young lady and saw her attempts to make me over as threatening. Although it was certainly not my grandmother's intention, to me she seemed like Pat without the whippings. We had become strangers, so I had lost her too.

I was on my own in my new high school in Michigan. I asked the teachers to look at me when they were speaking so I could read their lips, but they would forget and start talking while writing on the blackboard. I tried to stay busy and out of trouble, keeping up with my schoolwork. Sports were okay now that Pat wasn't around, so I eagerly joined the basketball team.

Years of not being able to hear speech had severely affected my own speech patterns, leaving me vulnerable to further teasing in school. I created an imaginary person and in my mind I became that person. I made up stories about myself to make others think I was important. I lied a lot and began believing my own lies. I began doing things to get attention, and when someone dared me to do something, I did it.

Warren and Pat had so thoroughly convinced me that my hearing problem was all in my head that I had long ago quit wearing my hearing aid. Warren repeatedly told me to stop playing dumb and to quit trying to get sympathy by pretending to be deaf. Rather than accept that I had hearing problems, he convinced himself that I was indeed retarded. Otherwise, in his mind, I would be talking and acting my age. Why, he wondered aloud, did he always have to use punishment to correct my behavior when he could easily talk and reason with my brothers?

I didn't want to let my father down. I wanted him to think I was normal, smart, and popular like my brothers. I wanted to make him forget that I was retarded, even though that was how I thought of myself. I spent as much time as possible practicing with the basketball team and became a good player. Because of my sports skills I began to gain some measure of acceptance, but still not the friends I so desperately wanted. I bragged about where we lived and what valuables we had in order to impress my peers.

In school it was a big deal to have a nickname. When I asked my brother what my nickname was, he replied half-jokingly, "Retard." One of the social skills I lacked was the ability to recognize a joke. I took him seriously and thought the word had a nice ring to it, not understanding the derogatory meaning. Then, in school, when I told others my nickname, they giggled and said it suited me perfectly. I thought they were paying me a compliment. I also lacked the ability to recognize sarcasm.

Soon everyone was calling me by my nickname instead of my real name and I felt good. When I walked down the halls at school and someone called out, "Hey, Retard," I'd smile and wave, happy to be recognized and accepted. I felt like I belonged and that my schoolmates wanted to be friends with me.

One day the teacher was taking attendance, calling out our names. When my name was called I raised my hand and corrected her, explaining that my name had been changed to "Retard." The classroom bubbled over with giggles. I was confused when the teacher told me it wasn't a nice word.

When I got home I tried to look up "retard" in the dictionary but couldn't find it. When my brother came home later, I asked him what it meant, but he wouldn't answer me. When I asked my grandmother, all she would say was that it wasn't a nice word. When I couldn't get anyone to tell me the meaning, I decided it was worth the attention I was getting and kept the nickname.

Only when I played basketball did I feel almost normal. I was a few years older than most of the other players on the team and one of the best players. Typically I walked the short quarter mile home after the games. Once, when the game was over at 8:30 P.M. and I was supposed to be home by 9 P.M., I didn't arrive until 4 in the morning. I had a seizure and passed out, and upon awakening disoriented, began walking in the wrong direction. I wandered around in suburbs I had never seen, and when it began to rain, I curled up, exhausted, on someone's porch and slept. When the family dog licked my face, I left quickly, afraid the family would call the police.

I eventually found my street. My father had called the police then gone to bed. My poor, shaken grandmother, who had waited up all night, let me in when I banged on the door. It was almost daylight when I went to bed without cleaning up, and my grandmother let me sleep most of the day. Warren was sure I'd been out partying and was very upset with me. He didn't believe my story about being lost and threatened to send me to live with Pat if I didn't straighten up.

The idea of having to live with Pat was terrifying. I stopped all sports and became a hermit. Pulling away from others was my natural response to threats or painful experiences. If I was out of sight, I thought, I'd also be out of mind—there would be no accidents, no wrong behavior, no seizures. It was terribly boring to stay in my room when I could look out the window and see other kids playing softball. Yet the instant I made up my mind to leave my hermit stage, I'd become terribly afraid of making the wrong move. I did *not* want to be sent back to live with Pat.

So as soon as I came home from school I went to my room and stayed there until dinner. After dinner I returned to my room and stayed there until breakfast. I didn't want any more blackouts, whether they were real or my imagination. I even avoided the other kids at school, keeping to myself to limit the teasing. The other kids took great delight in mimicking my habit of swaying back and forth to calm myself and, try as I might, I couldn't break it.

My grandmother was very worried. She couldn't understand why I didn't want to be around my family and why I had no friends. Thinking a pet might help, she asked Warren to get me a puppy from the Humane Society. He found Jiffy, a German shepherd and a cockapoo mix. In the wonderful way of animals, she loved me unconditionally. I fed her, walked and brushed her, and treated her like my child. Every minute I wasn't in school I spent with Jiffy. She responded only to me. She was only allowed in the recreation room and never on the furniture, so I spent all my free time on the floor with her there.

I began having blackouts more frequently. I hid in my room so Warren wouldn't know. I was afraid that if I caused trouble by having to go to the doctor when nothing wrong was wrong with me, he would send me back to Stoutamyre or to live with

Pat. The only time I left my room was to go to school, but I always stopped by the recreation room to brush Jiffy and tell her how much I loved her.

During my self-imposed isolation, I started a journal. I had tried telling people in my family a little bit about Stoutamyre as I gradually learned that what happened there didn't happen to every child. But they told me the stories were hard to believe, and I could tell they thought I was inventing the stories to get attention. I knew what had really happened though, and I felt better telling my journal about it, since my family wouldn't listen. So I began my journal with my earliest memories and continued until it was current. I needed a record of all that had happened to me. When Peter caught me writing in my journal, he tried to talk me out of keeping one, saying that I needed to look to the future. But I kept writing.

Finally accepting the fact that I needed some help with my speech—and with none available at my high school—Warren enrolled me in a communication skills program at Eastern Michigan University in Ypsilanti. I began attending weekly speech classes. Sue, the speech therapist, was one of the most patient people I have ever met and knew exactly how to calm and encourage me. She helped me concentrate on making smooth sentences that made sense. With her help, I tape-recorded my voice and used the hearing aid to listen to myself speak. The hardest sounds were *s*, *ch*, *sh*, and *r*, and when I tried to avoid words with those sounds, Sue stopped me and made me use them. It took several years, but Sue turned me into a talking person.

Not having the motivation to exercise on my own, I began an aerobics class at the YMCA to stay in shape after quitting the basketball team. One of the instructors was a group leader at a summer camp in Chelsea, Michigan, for children with he-mophilia. Thinking it might be a good idea to be away from my father for a while and spend time with other people, I volunteered.

I helped out in the kitchen, setting and clearing the table and doing dishes for part of each day, and in the afternoons I played lawn games with the children. I enjoyed the work, both in the kitchen and playing with the children, but soon began to hunger for some of the attention the younger kids were receiving. One day I cut my finger just so the nurse would mother me, but I wanted more. Another time I pretended to pass out near the lake and had the whole camp in an uproar. When I wasn't contacted to volunteer the next year, I guessed that they had figured out that I was just playing games.

Because of my great desire for popularity, I became involved with the wrong crowd. I would have walked on burning coals for a few words of praise or a pat on the back, so when they told me to take something from someone else, I did it. They always told me that what I had taken really belonged to them and that I was just returning it, so it wasn't really stealing. They told me that they liked me, that I was their good friend.

One day we were sitting outside at lunch. I was feeling great, better than in a long time because I had friends. Another girl from one of my classes took me aside and told me that my friends were not a good group to hang out with. She said to be careful because they were just using me. When I told the others, they said that she was just jealous because I had friends and she didn't. Not wanting to lose the only friends I had, I believed them. If someone gave me a hard time, they said, the group would stick up for me. If someone made fun of my speech or the way I rocked, the group would take care of him. No one gave me any trouble while I was part of this group.

One afternoon after school we walked to a nearby park. As we all sat around on the grass, relaxing in the sun, one of the girls pulled a plastic bag from her backpack. Inside was a small packet of white papers and something that looked like the herbs my grandmother put in spaghetti. She laid her notebook on the grass, placed one of the small papers on it, and carefully put some of the herb on the paper, expertly rolling it up into a tight cylinder and twisting the ends together. She took a match from her pocket and lit it, producing a strange-smelling smoke.

Curious, I watched as each of them took turns putting it in their mouths, holding their breaths, and coughing and laughing as they blew out smoke. I had never seen anything like it before and asked what it was. One girl told me it was a joint and asked if I smoked. I lied and said that I did it all the time, that I had lots of the same stuff at home. Everyone stood around watching as I took my first puff.

The cough that doubled me over convinced them that I had been lying. I would have to pay to get back in their good graces. From home, I took money, jewelry, trophies, musical instruments, and anything else that seemed of value and put it in a box to take to my friends. They were happy; I was their friend again. After that, anytime they got mad at me I would steal (coats, gloves, lunches) for them as a way to re-earn their friendship.

Eventually I got caught. The principal called Warren into his office and told him about the thefts and the crowd I was associating with. I knew what Pat would have done but she wasn't there. Warren didn't whip me, but his threat to send me back to Stoutamyre and leave me there forever had the desired effect.

Again, the change was immediate and dramatic. I began working harder in school, spending more time on my homework and consequently getting better grades. I changed the way I dressed, began to use better speech, and gave up the false friends. I set new goals for myself. When I was in the eleventh grade and nearly twenty years old, I got my first job as a dishwasher in a restaurant at the Sears store in the Briarwood Mall.

At the beginning of my senior year in high school, I suddenly realized that I needed to decide what I wanted to do after I graduated. I knew I wanted to go to college like my brothers had, and I wanted people to think I was smart. At a career fair offered by the school, I found myself drawn to hospitals and health-related programs. To learn more about working in a hospital, I started taking a bus to the University of Michigan Hospital after my morning classes.

The first thing I noticed was that the staff wore white jackets. One day, while in the basement, I found a jacket in a laundry hamper. I picked it up and tried it on. A patch on the side read "Respiratory Therapist." I didn't know what that meant but it didn't matter; I looked like everyone else. I started going to each floor to visit with the patients. I would go behind the nurses' desk and pick up a chart, pretending that I worked there. Today, with increased security and photo ID badges, this never would have worked, but at that time, no one questioned who I was or why I was there.

I went to the hospital every day after school, wearing my white jacket. As I wandered the halls I blended in with the variety of people who made up the population of the teaching hospital. During my months of observations, I experienced the smell, the fear, and the joy of a hospital and wished that I worked there.

Everyone was nice to me and no one ever made fun of my speech. My greatest joy came from visiting the patients, and comforting them by just being there. I let them talk, even though most of the time I didn't know what they were saying. They talked too fast for me to speechread, but I just went along, agreeing with everything they said. Eventually this practice got me in trouble.

After ten or fifteen "yeah's" and "uh-huh's," I finally said, "Yeah," at the wrong time. The woman had just asked me if she was going to die. Without knowing what she had said, I continued on with my "yeah's," and she began screaming. A nurse came in to calm her down and later asked me why I had told her that she was going to die. When I realized what the woman had asked me and how I had responded, I became so upset that I stopped visiting patients for a while.

The children's ward was safer. There, I watched the kids play with stuffed animals and toys that I had never seen before. One afternoon I walked into the play area and sat down next to a young girl, who proudly showed me the stuffed animal her mother had brought for her birthday. My hands shook as I reached out for it, remembering all the mangled, destroyed teddy bears of my childhood. I thought about tearing it up, but seeing the look of love on her face, I knew I couldn't. A few days later I went to her room when she was sleeping, picked up the teddy bear, and sat down in the rocking chair by her bed. I don't know how long I sat there, petting and hugging the bear as tears streamed down my face, but gradually my fear went away. I no longer wanted to destroy it. I asked my grandmother for some money and bought one for myself. Holding my own bear felt good.

I began to realize that I wasn't going to the hospital to learn about healing others; I was going to heal myself. It had already helped a great deal, and I gradually began visiting the hospital less and less often.

When school was nearly out I made one last trip to the hospital and retraced all my steps, reliving the memories of the past months. I returned the white jacket to the laundry chute where I had found it and said good-bye to the hospital. I had only a few months until graduation and I knew what I wanted to do. Working in a hospital became my goal.

9

Life at home didn't get any worse, but it didn't get better either. I wanted to learn how to do things around the house—how to cook, clean, and do laundry—but my grandmother always said she could do it faster herself. Perhaps she was afraid that if I learned how to do what she did, we would no longer need her. Warren spent his free evenings deep in conversation with Peter, who was going to a nearby college. They discussed everything from girls, to managing money, to Peter's education. I was the retarded daughter who couldn't learn; therefore, I was unworthy of my father's time.

In the late afternoons and on weekends I went to my job as a dishwasher. I always signed on for extra hours on holidays or if someone was out sick. I had nothing else to do with my time, and I wanted to save money to buy a car and pay for my college tuition. Warren refused to pay my way through college and repeatedly told me that I wasn't capable of living alone, taking care of myself, owning a car, or attending college. If anything, his insistence that I would never be able to live independently only served to spur me on. I told myself that if my brothers could do these things, then so could I. I took a driver's training class for the school's special education population who were able to learn to drive; I passed, and got my driver's license. So much for that "can't."

For a long time I had relied on the bus system. But now that I had my driver's license, owning a car would make it easier to get to and from work. I took the money I'd saved (more than $1,200) to the nearest car dealership, spotted a lovely, dark blue Volkswagen Beetle, and paid for it with cash. I had enough money left over for the license plate and for the first six months' insurance. There went another "can't."

I drove my car home and parked it in the driveway, making sure I left enough room for Warren's car. I walked into the house and greeted my grandmother with a huge grin and told her that my first car was in the driveway, expecting her to be pleased for me. Not quite sure if I was joking or not, she looked out the window. Her expression turned grim as she said, "Your father won't be too happy about this. You should have spoken to him first."

"But I worked hard to earn money to buy my own car," I said, guiltily, beginning to feel less like a grown-up and more like a little kid.

When Warren came home, I met him at the door with smiles. I told myself he would be proud of me for working so hard and saving my money.

"Whose car is in the driveway?" he asked.

"Mine," I beamed.

"Quit joking, Anne. It's been a long day and I'm in no mood for teasing. Who's here?" he said tensely.

"Nobody is here, I'm not teasing, and it is *my* car," I said, trying to keep the smile on my face from fading.

When he finally realized that I wasn't joking and that I really had bought a car, he got mad, saying that I wasn't capable of making responsible decisions, much less owning and caring for a vehicle.

"How come my brothers can own cars and move out?" I asked, no longer able to keep the hurt from my voice. "I'll be graduating from high school soon, and I want to go to college."

"That's absolutely out of the question, Anne!" he shouted. "You may as well face it—you're not going to move out, go to college, or own your own car, and that's final!"

"Yes, I will! You'll see," I sobbed, as I turned and ran to my room. I didn't know how, but I would find a way to get out on my own. And the Beetle? Well, it served me well for many years.

I became friends with Ruth Warner, one of the cooks at the restaurant, and began going to church with her and her husband Glenn. They often invited me to their house for dinner, and at Christmas, Ruth gave me a present. She handed it to me at work, and at first I didn't know how to respond. Even though I had been feeling closer to Ruth and Glenn, I was suddenly overcome with shyness and didn't even remember to say, "Thank you," as my grandmother had taught me.

"Go ahead and open it," Ruth said, smiling. It took me a while to work up the courage to do so, but finally I carefully removed the ribbon and peeled away the tape. Inside the box were a blue skirt and a white blouse that Ruth had made for me.

Nervously I tried to smile as I went in the locker room to try on the new clothes. Once inside, I closed the door and leaned against it, trying to get control of my emotions. I wanted more than anything to destroy the outfit so I wouldn't have to wear it. Frantically I looked around the locker room but saw nothing that would help me. I knew Ruth and the others were on the other side of the door waiting to see what I looked like in the new clothes. I wanted the floor to open up and swallow me. I wanted a bolt of lightning to sear through the roof and strike me down—anything so I wouldn't have to put on the new skirt and blouse.

My mind was flooded with memories of Pat trying to dress me as a young lady, and all the beatings that followed when I objected. I wanted to leave on the baggy jeans and jacket that I was comfortable in, but I knew Ruth would be hurt. Since Ruth had never met Pat there was no way she could have known how this would affect me. She had shown me nothing but friendship and kindness—the very things I had been starving for—and I didn't want to lose that. Gritting my teeth and fighting back the tears, I slipped off the jeans and jacket and put on the skirt and blouse. My heart was thudding as I opened the door and stepped out to show them what they wanted to see. I smiled politely at their compliments, but I was still uneasy.

I took the skirt and blouse to Ruth's when I stayed with them on weekends, and I wore the outfit to church, trying to block out the memories of Pat. Ruth was very different from Pat, and she never tried to force me to do anything, preferring to teach appropriate behavior by example.

June 12, 1975. Graduation day at Pioneer High School. Our school used the University of Michigan football stadium across the street for graduation ceremonies and as I sat in the vast bowl of the stadium waiting for my diploma, all I could think was, *Now what?*

All around me conversations buzzed about who was going to which college and when. The fresh young faces were filled with excitement as they told me of college or job plans—some were going to work in their parents' companies. I, on the other hand, had no plans.

Motivation wasn't the problem; I had plenty of that. What I lacked was emotional and financial support from my family, since Warren steadfastly refused to even *loan* me the money for a college education. All of my brothers were either in college or had already graduated and were well on their way to successful careers. Repeatedly I asked why he refused to help me and his answer was always the same: because I was unable to manage alone.

The only way I knew to prove that I could live away from home was to do it. It wasn't what I had originally planned to do upon graduating, but feeling depressed and without a future, I moved in with Ruth and Glenn.

Warren disliked the Warners even before he met them and he especially didn't like the idea of my moving in with them. I wasn't certain whether he was angry because he would no longer be able to control me or because I had shown strength he hadn't known I possessed.

Living with Ruth and Glenn wasn't enough. I was still a full-time dishwasher; the only difference was that I drove to another home in the evenings. I wanted more out of life; I wanted an education. I talked with everyone I knew until I found a way to go to college. The first step, I learned, was to contact Michigan Vocational Services, an organization that arranges for education and job placements for people with handicaps. Taking this route was difficult for me because I didn't consider myself handicapped. However, according to the state of Michigan, my hearing loss qualified me for the program. I finally accepted this as the opportunity I needed to get a college education so I could begin my career in medicine.

Through this program the state government was going to pay my tuition to a college for deaf and hard of hearing students. The school was in Rochester, New York and I was frightened by the idea of moving so far away. Yet I knew I couldn't pass up this opportunity. Once I made the decision to apply I began to get excited—I was going to college after all!

When the application form arrived, I didn't know the answers to some of the questions and I didn't want to call my father for help. I didn't want him to know of my plans to go to college, and I didn't need to hear his negativity. When I explained the situation to my counselor at the Michigan Vocational Rehabilitation Center he agreed to call my father himself and get the necessary information. With the forms filled out and sent in, all that was left to do was work and wait.

After I was accepted, I called to tell my father that I was going to college. His first words were, "How much will it cost and who's going to pay for it?" When I told him that the state was paying, he sneered, "It'll never work. Where will you stay?" He wasn't going to have to pay for it, but he still wasn't happy for me. The Warners and my grandmother encouraged me to go for it, though, and I went anyway.

The National Technical Institute for the Deaf (NTID) had a month-long orientation program in the summer, and I drove to Rochester by myself. The campus was very new, with a mix of both deaf and hearing students. "Culture shock" is much too mild a term for what I experienced at NTID.

I was completely on my own for the first time in my life. I had an academic advisor to help me select classes, but the school didn't provide anyone like Miss Nancy to help me negotiate the social aspects of school. Having no idea how to act, I reverted to my old, attention-getting ways. I was rude and impatient and interrupted everyone. I belched and passed gas, which had always been good for a laugh in high school but here only made me unpleasant to be around. When conflicts arose I fell apart, running to the person in charge to help me handle them. Something as simple as being unable to find a book was cause for a breakdown.

I had what I had wanted for so long, but I didn't know what to do with it. One thing was certain: I no longer wanted to be on my own. I was desperately lonely and all my childish attempts to call attention to myself only succeeded in alienating those around me. In an effort to communicate with the other students, I began to learn American Sign Language, but not even the new language could make up for my social deficits.

I had signed up to study to be a medical technician, but my poor eyesight created problems with the microscope and I became discouraged. I couldn't achieve my original goal and I stubbornly refused to choose an alternative.

I had no idea what to do with my free time, jealously watching the others who knew how to interact with each other. My roommate was also deaf. This was her first time away from home, too, but all she wanted was to sleep all day and party all night. On the nights when she wasn't partying, she usually had someone sneak into our dorm room after curfew and they would stay up all night laughing and signing.

When I tried to make friends with people who didn't have hearing problems, I pretended to be unable to talk in order to get extra attention. I wanted them to accept me and at the same time feel sorry for me. My game worked until one day I spoke without thinking and gave myself away.

To satisfy my limitless need for reassurance, I called Ruth and Glenn every day—collect—leaving them with an extremely high telephone bill. In my continuing effort to prove to Warren that I could live without his help, I chose not to call him.

When I completed the orientation period and returned home to Ruth and Glenn, I realized that I wasn't emotionally ready for the path I had chosen. The social difficulties and the inability to pursue my dream of working in medicine were enough to persuade me not to return to NTID in the fall. I needed the security of familiar people and surroundings in order to function. Although unwilling to admit that Warren was right, I secretly wondered if maybe I *was* retarded and would never be able to live independently. My next plan was to continue to live with the Warners while going to school during the day and working odd jobs at night.

One of my jobs was at a small airport, cleaning out the airplanes and hangars, and I was very happy there. The pilots and mechanics at Butler Aviation accepted me for who I was and never made fun of my speech. I was the only female employee there, and my coworkers went out of their way to make me feel like I was one of them. In addition to my regular duties, they taught me how to move the planes in and out of the hangars, how to enter information in the logbooks, and how to fuel the airplanes. The vibration of the engines, which everyone else wore earplugs to protect against, felt good to me. Watching the planes taxi down the runway and lift off into the air, I felt a sense of freedom, as though I were flying along with the plane. I even loved the smell of aviation fuel that permeated my clothes at the end of the day.

As luck would have it, I met someone who worked in the personnel department at General Motors (GM) who asked if I would be interested in working there. I wasn't; I wanted to work in a medical profession, not a factory.

Before I ruled out working for GM, though, I told myself that I had to think rationally, that I needed the increase in salary to save enough money to go to college. I filled out the employment application, asking myself, *Who would hire me, anyway?* Within a week I received a call to come in for a physical and an interview with the person in charge of hiring people with disabilities. I almost turned down the job at GM because of the sense of camaraderie I felt at Butler Aviation. Yet I resisted the urge to decline the job offer, and a few days later I was a GM employee.

The work environment at GM was the exact opposite of Butler Aviation. Both men and women of all ages and races worked at the plant. In the first department I was assigned to, I worked mostly with women. The first few days weren't so bad as they tried to get to know me. Even though my social skills were still very poor and I didn't know how to conduct myself in public, I tried to be friendly with everyone and waited to see who would be friendly with me.

Working around the mechanics at Butler Aviation, I had adopted many of their habits, as I had adopted the habits of my brothers in the past. They wore dirty clothes—I wore dirty clothes. They came to lunch with dirt under their nails and on their arms, so that must be OK. Often their shirttails were out, so mine were too. No one tried to make me behave any differently. It wasn't a problem until I started to work with women.

I came to work every day wearing the same clothes, without showering or washing or combing my hair. When the other women questioned me about this, I didn't know how to answer them, thinking that it had nothing to do with my job. In their own way they were trying to help me, but I misunderstood their intentions, seeing their questions as just more attempts to make me over into someone I wasn't.

The daily work routine of two breaks and an hour for lunch was very uncomfortable. I didn't want to leave my work area because I feared interacting with my coworkers. I didn't know how to act around them, and they spoke so rapidly that I had trouble following their conversations. I particularly dreaded lunchtime. I didn't know where to sit or with whom and usually ended up eating my lunch sitting on the bathroom floor.

When I received my first paycheck, I didn't know what to do with it. I hadn't needed much spending money before, so I used to give my paychecks to my father. A coworker, only half jokingly, said to sign my paycheck over to her. Having been beaten into submission throughout my childhood, I had learned my lesson well and was accustomed to obeying without question; I turned the check over, signed my name as she told me, and handed it to her.

Word spread throughout the plant, and soon others were coming to me on payday asking for my check. I enjoyed having so many friends at my new job. When I began to have financial troubles and was unable to pay rent, Glenn helped me open a checking account and taught me how to deposit my checks and pay bills. My new "friends" quickly disappeared.

After being in the department with mostly women for a while, I was transferred to one with only male employees. At no time since I had been wearing my hearing aid and reading lips had I been exposed to the slang or swear words that were common in that department. Conversations at Butler Aviation had been about fishing, cars, motorcycles, current events, and technical aspects of the airplanes. At my new job, all talk centered on sex. I had never heard racist or sexist jokes before, so I didn't know when to laugh at their jokes. When I asked the meaning of the four-letter words or the sexual terminology, I was laughed at for not already knowing.

Once during lunch, I watched four male coworkers deep in conversation. I saw one of them say the phrase "blow job," and I tried to figure out the meaning by taking the two words apart and assigning a definition to each one: "blow" which refers to air and "job" meaning a work assignment. I came to the conclusion that this phrase referred to the use of an air hose to clean debris or metal chips out of a transmission part, and that a position for this type of work had become available. It occurred to me that I might be allowed to do something different for a while so I walked over to their table and asked if they thought I would be qualified to do the "blow job." Their expressions of surprise quickly changed to raucous, red-faced laughter as they all got up and left without answering.

I couldn't figure out why they were laughing; I had asked a serious question. Since people often laughed at my speech, I thought maybe that was it. I went over the question in my head to make sure I had pronounced everything correctly so that when I asked someone else, I wouldn't get laughed at. I rehearsed my question a few times before asking another group.

I walked up to them, confident that I would say the sentence correctly, and asked, "Where can I apply for the blow job position?" This group went crazy! As they laughed, some of them doubled over with tears running from their eyes. After my third try with the same results, I gave up and went home to ask Glenn. He was shocked but didn't laugh at me. Instead he explained that "blow job" referred to a sexual act, and that my coworkers were making fun of my question. I was so embarrassed that I didn't want to go to work the next day and when I did, I found that the story of my question had circulated around the plant, making me the brunt of a new type of joke.

One woman from a nearby department knew about me from rumors. The first time we met she wanted to know why I wasn't married. *Am I doing something wrong by not being married?* I wondered. She then asked if I was a lesbian. When I asked if that was a dirty word, she said no, that it was a nice word, one to be proud of. She didn't look like she was teasing me and I liked the sound of the word, so I agreed with her, thinking she was paying me a compliment. She said that she wanted to be my friend, and that friends used nicknames, didn't they? Proud and full of confidence, I thought I had finally made a good friend after all. I told everyone that I was a lesbian and that I had a friend. Why were they laughing at me again? Thinking that perhaps I wasn't pronouncing the word correctly, I found the woman again and asked her to repeat it and asked her why the others were laughing. She said that they were jealous and wanted to be brave and smart like I was but didn't have the guts. Of course, I believed her.

When I went home that afternoon and told Glenn that I had made a new friend and that I was a lesbian he collapsed in a chair. I told him the whole story and watched his anger build — anger at the woman, not at me. When he told me the real meaning of the word, I was hurt; this woman, who I thought wanted to be my friend, was just as bad as the men were. Glenn told me not to trust the people at work, and if there was a word I needed to know the meaning of, to ask him.

When I left my father's house and moved into the Warners' mobile home, it was with the idea that I was getting a new family that really cared for me. I began calling Glenn, "Pop" and

Ruth, "Mom." I became Glenn's shadow, following him everywhere he went. He seldom yelled at me, encouraged me to go to school, and taught me how to do things. Under Glenn's gentle tutoring I learned how to use power tools safely, change the oil in a car, and do other repairs. Glenn worked the midnight shift at a Ford plant, and I often met him for breakfast and a walk to the park. As we walked and fed the squirrels, he talked to me about the Bible and taught me the story of Jesus and his life. Amazed that I had never seen a Bible, Glenn and Ruth bought one for me to take to church on Sundays and to Bible study on Wednesday nights.

I knew nothing of the basics of family relationships and as a result, nearly destroyed Ruth and Glenn's. At the same time I was growing closer to Glenn, I was pulling away from Ruth. She made me skirts for church and encouraged me to wear them with panty hose. Why couldn't I just go in the comfortable clothes I was used to? I began to be afraid she wanted to take over where Pat left off. My experiences with Pat and Margie had caused me to distrust all women, and I didn't want to be like any of them. All the ones I had met had been the same—talking, thinking, and acting alike—and I had no interest in their gossip, jewelry, or clothes. Glenn, on the other hand, accepted me as I was; he listened to me and acknowledged that I existed.

Even though Glenn and Ruth's children were all grown and living on their own, jealousy and confusion soon developed over my role in the household. None of us was communicating very well. I was unaware that to others, I appeared to be dating a married man. The better Glenn and I got along, the more uncomfortable Ruth became with the idea that I was spending so much time with her husband. Whether in fact or in my imagination, I viewed Ruth more and more like Pat and felt safer with Glenn. He felt more like a father than my real father did.

In 1979, after nearly four years, I moved out of Ruth and Glenn's home and bought a mobile home in the same park. This served to remove me from what was becoming an uneasy situation, and also to increase my feelings of independence—and my vulnerability to false friends.

10

Not long after I moved out of the Warners' home, I met a young woman named Linda who had a seven-year-old son. Large boned and blonde, she was always telling jokes and seemed full of energy and fun. When we decided to be roommates I moved out of my mobile home, but kept up the payments. I held on to the home as a security blanket, so I would always have someplace to go if things didn't work out with Linda and her son, Jerry. I wasn't good at managing my money and I never considered renting it out; all I could think about was finally being part of a real family.

The three of us moved into a large house in Ypsilanti, just ten minutes from my job. Linda was a registered nurse and worked the day shift in a nursing home nearby. Ruth had taught me how to cook, and I always had a meal ready for Linda and her son before I went to work in the afternoons at GM.

We had been living together for about six months when I returned from work one Friday evening to find the house filled with Eastern Michigan University students. Linda was having a party. The living room window was open a crack but the room was filled with smoke. I remembered the smell from my high school days. I walked into the kitchen and saw a guy with a cake pan filled with a pile of dried up plants. The marijuana smoke was making me feel funny so I went outside. As I was getting in my car to leave, Linda ran out to try to stop me, saying that I would get used to the smell.

I spent the night at Glenn and Ruth's house and returned home the next morning to a mess: broken glass on the porch, cigarette burns on the carpet, dirty glasses and beer cans everywhere, and chips and cheese melted onto the stove. I went to wake Linda up and found a strange woman, who claimed to be the baby-sitter, in her bed. There had been a raid the night before, she told me, and the police had taken everyone away. I swept the porch, washed the dishes, and wiped off the stove. I couldn't do much about the cigarette burns in the carpet, so when I had cleaned up as best I could, I went to work. Two days later Linda returned from jail and the landlord evicted us, keeping the security deposit to pay for the carpet. I was beginning to wonder about Linda's behavior but believed her when she said that everybody smoked dope. I agreed to keep being her roommate, and we rented an apartment together.

That summer Linda was gone a lot, working double shifts, so I looked after her son until the baby-sitter relieved me to go to work. One afternoon Jerry cut his foot on a piece of glass in the yard and a neighbor volunteered to take him to the hospital while I called Linda. I looked through her room until I found her work number but the man who answered said that Linda had been fired months before. She returned home a few days later, saying that she had been transferred, and left me a new emergency number. When I confronted her, she said that her old boss was jealous of her promotion.

Linda's friends often stayed the night. Once, when I had borrowed my brother's sleeping bag for a camping trip, promising to take good care of it, a couple of her friends asked to borrow it. When I told them no, that it wasn't mine, they accused me of being selfish, so I reluctantly agreed. The next day I found the sleeping bag torn into pieces. Linda laughed, saying how funny it was that they both tried to fit in the sleeping bag at the same time. "Stop crying like a baby," she said. "You can always go to the store and get another one." When I told her that her friends owed me money for the new sleeping bag, she said it wouldn't be polite to ask them since it had been an accident.

Linda said she wanted me to be normal and to have a good time, so she took me to a bar she frequented. As we walked in she said, "You look good. Handle yourself sexy, stay at the bar until closing, pick up a guy, and take him home. Make breakfast for him and then you get your reward: he'll take you to bed." I didn't want to do it—go to the bar *or* go to bed with a guy. But I didn't want to be alone either. I needed friends. Linda went to bars and went to bed with guys and she had friends. . . . I took a deep breath and went into the bar.

Before I knew it a guy was right next to me, whispering in my ear. I couldn't hear him, but not wanting him to think I was abnormal, I didn't tell him I had a hearing problem. He thought I was playing hard to get when all I really wanted was for him to go away and find another woman.

The bar was overheated and packed with people, and I was thirsty. He brought me a drink that looked like the Coke I had asked for, and I drank it down in one gulp before I realized that it was more than just Coke. I began to feel and act silly.

When the bar was closing, the man let me know he wanted to go home with me. Linda was all smiles when we went to the bathroom before leaving. She said I was about to get my reward. Linda had picked up someone and she drove the four of us home. I was not happy. I prayed for a car accident that would send me to the hospital.

As Linda and I made breakfast, she popped some pills in her mouth and asked if I wanted some speed. I told her, "No thanks."

It was 4 A.M. when we finished breakfast. I volunteered to do the dishes, thinking to postpone what was supposed to come next, but Linda laughed as she and her date went to her room, saying that the dishes could wait until morning.

Even though I was really sleepy, I sat down to watch TV, trying to avoid the man sitting on the couch next to me. I recoiled when he began to touch me, and I stood up to leave the room. He grabbed my wrist and pulled me down. He was clearly too strong for me, and I started to cry. He pushed me to the floor and climbed on top of me, pushing my panties down with one hand while he fumbled with his zipper with the other. I gave up, thinking that if he got what he had come for he would leave. I was too tense for him to even force entry, though, and eventually he left in frustration.

I fell into an exhausted, grateful sleep on the living room floor. When Linda woke me up to ask if I had gotten "lucky," I lied and said yes. That made her happy. In Linda's opinion, anyone who didn't pick up a man for sex every night must be a lesbian.

Before I met Linda, all I knew about sex came from classes in school. Linda took it upon herself to reeducate me. She showed me X-rated movies to turn me on so that I'd have sex with the men she brought to the house. The movies had the opposite effect, however, and I would hide in my room, sick and afraid. It's easy now to look back and see that she was using me, but in my extreme social innocence I desperately wanted to believe that she was my friend.

After a while Linda gave up on bringing men home, preferring to do her partying elsewhere and leave me to take care of Jerry. When I tried to get out of baby-sitting, she told me that when we had moved in together I had agreed to take on family responsibilities. I transferred to the day shift so I could watch her son after school and on weekends. Linda's car broke down, and she began driving mine. When I told her we should get a second car so I could have mine back, she said that money was too tight.

I was becoming extremely frustrated and Jerry missed his mother. All three of us began getting on each other's nerves.

One night after struggling to get Jerry to sleep, I dozed in front of the TV. He woke up and began running around the apartment. When he screamed as loudly as he could in my ear, I reacted by picking him up and throwing him across the room. Luckily he wasn't hurt. Horrified at what I had done, I made up my mind to tell Linda that I didn't want to watch him anymore.

The next morning I woke up to discover Linda wasn't there and neither was my car. I got Jerry ready for school and walked him to the bus stop, then called my boss to ask for help getting to work. The next day I asked the neighbor to take Jerry to school so I could leave early enough for the forty-five minute walk to work. Three days later, Linda's sister sat with Jerry while her mother took me to Chelsea Hospital without explaining why. She led me to a private room where Linda lay in the bed. She had been in a wreck and my car was totaled.

Later that day I went to the bank to withdraw money for the down payment on another car, but was told that I had no money. How could that be? I had faithfully deposited all but a few dollars of every paycheck. The bank manager handed me a statement showing a *debt* of $6,000! Impossible! Where had my money gone? The sheet in my hand clearly showed my deposits every week but also withdrawals that I knew I hadn't made. At home I went over my checkbook, adding deposits and subtracting checks that I had written, but I could find no error. Linda hung up on me when I called her at the hospital to tell her of the problem.

The day Linda was released from the hospital I confronted her with my frustration. I told her I was tired of walking to and from work and tired of taking care of Jerry. I not only had no money or car, but also a great deal of debt. Then she told me her story.

She was not a registered nurse and, in fact, had been on welfare for several years. Instead of going to work each evening she had been going to the bars seven nights a week. On the nights she was supposedly working double shifts, she had gone home with men who paid her for sex. She would have been paid if I had had sex with the men she brought home—which explained why she was so angry when I wouldn't cooperate. She used the money, sometimes as much as $150 to $200 a night, to pay for drugs.

When prostitution was no longer enough to support her habit, she stole a pad of my checks, filled in whatever amount she needed, and cashed them at one of the bars. She had a friend at my bank who kept increasing the line of credit on my checking account. I had suspected nothing when, early in our friendship, she volunteered to handle the monthly bank statements. She had used *my* money to buy clothes and food and to pay *her* half of the rent! She had used *my* line of credit to pay off her old bills, leaving *her* debt-free. Anytime she treated me to dinner out or to special trips, it was with money she had taken from *my* checking account.

Jerry began sobbing when I went upstairs to pack my clothes. Linda argued that we were both adults—family members—and family didn't desert each other. Family stuck together and worked things out, she said. She said that Jerry would be devastated if I left, that he loved me like a sister. In the end I agreed to stay and to work overtime to pay off the debt, and she agreed to get a job and go to school to get her nursing degree. But before long she was back to her old ways, having men over to the house for sex. The last straw came when, in a drunken and drugged rage, Linda destroyed most of my belongings, including the journal I'd kept since high school. I packed my suitcase and went to stay with the Warners for a while before moving back into my mobile home. When I tried to take Linda to court, I learned that she had left the state. I never knew exactly how much money she had taken from me.

The pressure of trying to live in Linda's world and the work world at GM—of trying to fit into others' ideas of how I should be, act, and live my life—was taking its toll; my health began to deteriorate. In 1978 I began to have seizures again after being free of them for a long time. In addition to giving me a prescription, the doctor told me that according to the law once a person had a seizure, they couldn't operate a motor vehicle again until they had been seizure-free for six months. I felt as though my whole world had stopped. I became deeply depressed.

The doctors had difficulty adjusting my seizure medications. The phenobarbital made it hard to work; in fact, I was not allowed to work on cars. I was given paperwork to do in an office area away from the garage. Coworkers picked me up and took me home each day. When I was at home, I slept. It seemed that all I did was sleep, and when I was awake I felt as though I had a ton of bricks on my chest.

The correct dosage for the other drug, Dilantin, proved to be very difficult to determine and the doctors kept increasing it. Finally they replaced the Dilantin with Tegretol, which was much easier to regulate. After several months the seizures were finally under control.

Not being able to drive was more of a hardship on the weekends. Rides to and from work from my coworkers was one thing, but rides for socializing were harder to organize. When I began feeling better my father invited me up for a weekend. I agreed, thinking the time away would do me good. He would pick me up on Friday afternoon, he said, and bring me back on Sunday in plenty of time to arrange for a ride to work on Monday.

We arrived at his house in the early evening, and I went upstairs to freshen up before dinner. The volume of the television set told me that my grandmother was downstairs in her room. Her hearing had gotten worse since the last time I'd seen her, and her heart problems kept her on the main floor most of the time. As I stepped out of my room my father called to me from his room across the hall.

"Anne, come in for a minute," he said in a strange voice. He put his hand on the small of my back to guide me into the room. He began to talk, telling me that he had broken up with his latest girlfriend. I had never seen him so sad, so helpless. I was sitting on the edge of his bed, trying to read his lips and expressions to understand all that he was saying, when suddenly he stumbled toward me and pushed me back on the bed. Then I saw his red, puffy eyes and could smell alcohol on his breath.

I was so shocked that I couldn't even scream—not that it would have done any good. My mind went blank. What happened next is lost in a blur of pain and disbelief. I remember the bedroom window—wanting to jump out of it when he was finished with me.

The next thing I remember, I was in my room across the hall. I felt as though someone had picked me up and deposited me in another world, a world where foul deeds and evil smells were commonplace. I couldn't think. I felt numb and sick, filthy. It was hard to walk and harder to urinate. Somehow I slept; I woke the next morning trying to make myself believe it had been a nightmare. *My father did nothing to me; he loves me too much to hurt me. No father could do something like that to his daughter.* It had to be the product of my stress-filled mind or the seizure medication. I would just try to forget about it. I must have been successful because I don't remember the rest of the weekend or the trip back home.

For weeks I could barely eat and kept to myself. I began missing work, staying home, filled with shame for dreaming such things. I didn't feel like I could talk to anyone about this. Even if it wasn't a nightmare, who would have believed me?

The next six months were hell. *Something must be terribly wrong with me,* I thought, *for my father to have done such a thing or for me to dream such a thing.* For a while I went to work but avoided my coworkers, convinced that they somehow knew my awful secret. Now they had good reason to make fun of me. After work I went home and slept. Part of me was in denial. With my family's help I had had plenty of practice convincing myself that I was retarded, that I didn't have a hearing problem, that Margie really loved me like a daughter. But then the reality came crashing down again. I held everything inside, refusing to talk to anyone, including Glenn and Ruth, even though I still lived in my mobile home near them.

I began to get sick. I had violent headaches and my eyes were sensitive to light. I had no appetite, and I vomited when I did eat. The doctor at the university hospital said my headaches were migraines and gave me a prescription for Darvon. When I took the Darvon I had no pain and felt really good. The Darvon even helped the despair and loneliness that had been my constant companion for years. I vowed never to let the prescription expire.

I was walking across the GM parking lot one day when a car came around the corner at full speed. I saw him coming straight toward me but had absolutely no fear. Others were shouting and waving, trying to get my attention, but I ignored them. I stood calmly, watching the car speed toward me. As the tires squealed and the car bounced to a stop one foot from me, I turned and continued across the parking lot.

A woman ran up to me screaming, "What's the matter with you, Anne? You could have been killed!"

To which I replied, "So?"

The migraines became so bad that the Darvon no longer helped and the nausea and vomiting increased. I went to stay with Ruth and Glenn for a while and ended up sleeping for three days. When Glenn came home the morning of the fourth day and saw that I still had not eaten, he became very angry.

"This has gone on long enough," he said. "I'm taking you to the hospital."

"Go away!"

"If you're not going to take care of yourself, then we'll have to take care of you. Now get dressed."

"I'll be okay. Just let me sleep a little longer," I said, my eyes slowly closing as I turned my back to him. I could ignore him if I couldn't see his face.

Not willing to give up without a fight, he walked to the other side of the bed. "No, you won't be okay. Not without help. Look at yourself. You're so thin; your color is awful. Now get dressed. Or am I going to have to dress you myself?"

"All right, all right," I replied weakly. "I'll get dressed. Just give me a few minutes."

Glenn drove me to the hospital where I was admitted immediately. According to their records I had lost nearly forty-five pounds. I was so dehydrated that the skin on my feet and elbows was cracking and my urine was a burnt orange color. Through their many tests the doctors determined that my illness wasn't physical, and they transferred me to the psychiatric unit at Chelsea Hospital in December 1980. There I was diagnosed with depression and a seizure disorder.

A few days after I arrived, when I had regained a little strength from the IVs, a nurse gave me a tour of the facilities. As we walked slowly down the hall, I caught part of what she said and asked her to repeat it so I could read her speech.

"We don't give shock treatments here," she said.

A ghost of a memory tried to surface. Shock treatments. Being strapped to a table with things on my head and a piece of something hard between my teeth. Where and when had this been done to me? Was it at Stoutamyre? I couldn't be sure. But I was sure that it had happened, and I felt a great relief that it wouldn't happen here.

During therapy sessions I learned that the nausea and vomiting were, in part, my response to stressful situations. Still hooked up to IVs, I attended both individual and group therapy sessions and slowly began to improve. I was able to open up and talk to the therapist about my difficult relationship with my family.

It took me a long time to talk about the rape, though. When the therapist started questioning me about my relationships with my father and brothers, I pulled back and refused to answer. I quickly changed the subject to something safer. After a number of such sessions, the therapist began to focus even more on my relationship with my family.

One day she wouldn't let me leave until I opened up. When I finally started to talk about what had been done to me, I was a disaster. The pain I felt was physical as well as emotional. I told the therapist about the beatings and the rape, and all of it came out in a flood of emotion. For the first time, I began to understand why headaches, stomach pains, vomiting, dizziness, self-hatred, and suicidal thoughts had taken over my life. I was completely overwhelmed.

On my way out of the room after the session, I paused in the doorway. "None of that really happened, though," I told her. "It was all a lie." I didn't want to believe that all those horrid things were actually true, and hoped that telling the therapist I had lied would make the pain and hurt go away. Maybe then the memories would no longer haunt me.

Eventually, I learned that my dependence on others often drove them away, and I practiced with the staff to develop more adult ways of relating to people. Yet as much as I progressed and learned to open up, I never talked about Stoutamyre. I simply told my therapist that I had "survived" my time there and would say nothing more.

I started attending substance abuse lectures and discovered that I had been too dependent on phenobarbital. With the neurologist's assurance that Dilantin would be sufficient to control my seizures, I threw away the phenobarbital.

When the nausea and vomiting stopped and my weight stabilized, the doctors began making plans for my discharge. At one point they recommended that I live in a halfway house or group home for a while, rather than live alone or with Ruth and Glenn. They felt that the Warners, probably unintentionally, had promoted my sense of dependency. In a group home the doctors thought that I could learn coping skills to help me function on my own. By the time I was ready to leave I felt much less depressed and more in control of my situation, and the doctors agreed to let me delay my decision about the group home. Arrangements were made with a therapist for outpatient visits.

11

Despite my progress in therapy, I still had a lot to learn. I was still looking for a family to replace the one that had never accepted me, and people who were willing to exploit me could still see my vulnerability.

As it turned out, staying in a group home never happened. Near the end of my five-week stay at Chelsea Hospital, a woman about my age walked over and sat at the table where I was drawing. Every time I looked up she was watching me. We began to talk, and I learned that she suffered from manic depression (now known as bipolar disorder). By the time I was discharged in January, Jean and I had become good friends. I returned a few days after my discharge to give her a ride home, and Jean invited me to stay with her and her two young sons. A month later I moved in with them, although I still kept my own mobile home in case things didn't work out.

Jean's rundown apartment was in a rough neighborhood on the northwest side of Ypsilanti. Most of the neighbors were on welfare, drugs, or both. We could hear loud music and fights through the thin walls. The odor of marijuana blew through the windows in the summer and drifted under the door in the winter.

Unable to work until her medication was adjusted, Jean was on welfare. At first we shared expenses, but I soon began paying for everything so she could have more money for herself and her boys. Jean taught me how to play the piano, to cook gourmet meals, to sew, and to dance. I taught her sign language and showed her about cars—I had been removing transmissions from vehicles at GM for almost four years by now, and it felt great to share my knowledge about cars. We joined a gym, worked on crafts, and had picnics. We had a nice life, or so I thought.

When Jean decided that she wanted to get rid of her old furniture but didn't have enough money to buy new, I brought most of mine from the trailer. She was always upset that she didn't have enough money to buy this or that, so I gave her money. Eventually I turned my paychecks over to her to pay the bills and buy groceries.

I wanted to get a degree in automotive mechanics, and Jean encouraged me to attend classes at Washtenaw Community College. She transcribed my tapes of the classes and helped me study for tests, and I began earning A's. I also attended workshops to learn more about manic depression and how to help Jean deal with it.

Because of her children, most of my activities with Jean centered on home. I began to realize that I was being used to fill the role of father to the two young boys, who seldom saw their dad. I taught them things that a father would typically teach his sons, like how to ride a bike and bait a hook. People who knew us assumed we were lesbians, probably because no one thought it was normal for two women to live together when one of them had children.

I had lived with Jean and her sons for about two years when I met Terry, a woman who also worked at GM. We had a lot in common and both enjoyed the outdoor activities I had been missing. As Terry and I became good friends, Jean became more and more jealous of the time we spent together.

I went home one day and told Jean that, although I still wanted to be friends, I was going to move out. She became furious, throwing chairs and screaming. Because of her outburst, I decided to stay, but often snuck out to meet Terry to go sailing or to basketball or hockey games. By making excuses and saying I was going somewhere else I avoided confrontations with Jean.

The next time I told Jean that I wanted to move out, she accused me of taking advantage of her. I reminded her that I had given her a lot of money: for food, clothes, baby-sitters, a car, gas, *and* I had paid the rent. When I left the apartment she was in tears, and I stayed for a while in my mobile home until loneliness and guilt drove me back to Jean's.

Glenn learned of my plight and arrived one day with several of his friends to help me move out. With Jean throwing pots and pans we managed to get only my clothes. I moved back into my almost-empty mobile home, and I never saw Jean or her boys again.

Sometime in the spring of 1981 I learned of testing that could be done at the University of Michigan to determine once and for all if I was retarded. I had an interview with Dr. DeYoung, the head of the neurology department, and he told me that I was most definitely not retarded. But that wasn't good enough for me; I wanted to take the formal test—to make it official, leaving no room for doubt. I had been called retarded for as long as I could remember, and just having the doctor say otherwise wasn't good enough. DeYoung told me that the test was expensive and my insurance wouldn't pay for it, but I didn't care; I would pay the $300 myself. I couldn't explain to him how important the results were to me. Finally, realizing that there was no point in trying to change my mind, he agreed to test me the following week.

I was ecstatic. I could barely sleep the night before my first day of testing. For three days I arrived at the hospital early in the morning and left in the afternoon. The tests consisted of comprehension questions and commonsense questions; they were very hard and often frustrating. In one section I had to remember as much as possible about what was said and then repeat it all back without stopping. I made sure they knew to face me so I could read their speech. When I was finished taking all the tests I had no idea how I would score.

Two weeks later, I sat at the table in the conference room as the doctors showed me my test results. The graph indicated that I had slightly above average intelligence. The doctors looked at me curiously, not fully comprehending the significance of what they had just given me. But there it was, in black and white: I was not retarded. I was not retarded! *I WAS NOT RETARDED!!*

I left the hospital with the memory of my place on the graph etched in my mind, a piece of paper with my test scores held tightly in my hand and my feet barely touching the ground. This was the biggest single day of my life. I was not retarded, and nothing else mattered. I knew from that day forward that if anyone said I was retarded, it wouldn't matter because I would know the truth. I rolled down the windows of my car as I began the long drive down the parking ramp and yelled, "I'm not retarded!" I told everyone I saw and didn't care if they looked at me strangely. I was too happy to care what other people thought. It was just a short time until my twenty-seventh birthday, and this was the best gift I could ever hope for.

All the way home I planned my next step—telling my father. In the year since our last encounter I had continued to try to convince myself that nothing had happened and for now this news was so important that I put it all behind me. Why had he worked so hard all those years to make me believe I was retarded? I thought the answer was obvious: He must have believed it himself. And if that were true, then surely he would be happy to learn he had been wrong—that his little retarded girl was really quite smart. I could hardly wait to tell him but it had to be in person. I had to see his face when I told him my news.

I was ready to get some answers to the questions that haunted me: Why was I sent to Stoutamyre? Didn't they love me anymore? Since I wasn't retarded, had I done something terribly wrong to cause them to send me away to a place like that? My brain was spinning with a whirling cloud of questions that demanded answers—answers that only a parent could give.

I called my father to tell him I was coming home for the weekend and that I had some exciting news to share. During the hour-long drive I rehearsed how I would tell him:

"Dad, last month I took some tests at U of M."

"What kind of tests, Anne? You're not sick again, are you?"

"No, Dad. These were intelligence tests."

"Now why would you want to put yourself through that?"

"Because I didn't think I was retarded, and I wanted to know for sure."

From that point on, my imagination failed me, for I had absolutely no idea what his response would be. I replayed the scene in my head but couldn't seem to take the conversation to the next level. I drove on, so caught up in my thoughts that the car must have driven itself as the scenery of midsummer Michigan slid by the window.

Between the time I had called and the time I arrived in Fenton, my father was called out of town on business. His quick departure was frustrating, although not unusual. When he left town on business, it was almost always at the last minute—and he rarely let people know when his plans suddenly changed. All my mental preparations for seeing him again and telling him my news had been wasted.

The moment had passed; I had wanted to see his reaction, to have him hug me and apologize for sending me away. But I still knew, and that was all that really mattered.

When I was about twenty-nine years old, Glenn and Ruth retired and moved to Florida, leaving a huge hole in my life. They had been my friends, my teachers, my sounding board, and my safety net for a long time. I was terribly lonely and began doing a lot of things with Terry and her friends. After I learned that the new insulation sprayed in the walls of my mobile home might cause cancer, I sold the trailer and moved in with Terry. We lived together for nearly three years but didn't see too much of each other. I had been transferred to a different department and we were both working a lot of overtime. In addition, Terry was taking classes at the local community college to become an electrician. I did the housework, the laundry, the ironing, and the cooking, and mowed the lawn in the summertime. I chose to do most of the work to allow Terry more time for homework and socializing with others. I had quit therapy some months earlier, convinced that I didn't need it; in fact, I was in denial.

During therapy I'd learned that I wanted a friend, but more than that, I wanted a mom—the kind of mom who would hug me and show that she cared for me. An acquaintance, observing my style of dress and apparent lack of femininity, introduced me to the gay community, thinking that I might be gay and not know it. Some of the lesbians I met were different from other women I'd known. They dressed like tomboys, just like me! I thought for sure that I would have no trouble finding a friend in this group. But no one wanted me for a friend; they were all looking for potential lovers and that wasn't the role I wanted. I was not gay, and this was not my kind of lifestyle.

Terry met a young man and moved out to live with him. Luckily I found an apartment and moved everything within two weeks. We had laughed together, cried together, gone camping and sailing and to the movies. I thought we had a good friendship, but we lost touch as soon as she moved out of the apartment.

I was on my own again. I went to parties, to bars, out dancing. I met a lot of different people but still couldn't find any happiness. I became depressed and often thought of ending my life. After all, what was life worth when there was no one to share it with?

I was drowning in my own despair when someone threw me a life ring. A hearing woman I hardly knew introduced me to a deaf club. As I walked into my first meeting, I was completely overwhelmed—I didn't know anybody and they were all signing so rapidly! I had been there only a few moments before an interpreter sat down with me, and we talked for hours. She helped me to realize that *I* wasn't the reason I didn't have friends; instead it was the type of people I was associating with, who didn't know how to relate to anyone who was different. She told me that this was very common in the deaf community. I wasn't totally deaf, but she explained that the community included people who were hard of hearing. *A community? Of people like me?*

The problem I was having, she said, was why deaf people choose to stay close to others who are deaf—they are uncomfortable with hearing people, who don't understand the rejection experienced by people who are deaf. She convinced me that I'd feel more comfortable trying to make friends with people in this community because I'd have more in common with them.

I left that first meeting feeling better than I had in a long time. This woman, this stranger, had literally saved my life. She had known exactly how I felt and what to say to help fill in a part of what had been missing in my life.

I brushed up on my sign language, developed some much-needed social skills, and was happy in the deaf club. I learned that I had a sense of humor and a gift for making people laugh, which made me happy, too. We were always going places and doing things as a group. In less than a year I was asked to become the president of the local chapter, but had to decline because of overtime at work.

Yet before long, I began to slip into my hermit's life. I lost my social connection with the deaf club because I spent so much time working and studying. Unable to organize my time effectively, I felt bad about giving up something that had made me very happy but I saw no way to make anything else fit into my days.

12

My father had dated plenty of women while he and Pat were separated, but not until he met Ann Callard did he ask Pat for a divorce. Ann was so much like Pat that she could have been a clone. Ann and Pat both drank to excess, drew attention to themselves in public, and had controlling personalities. They hated each other even before they were introduced and fought from the first time they met. The only apparent difference was that, as far as I know, Ann did not abuse the ten children she had from two previous marriages.

Warren and Ann were to be married in March 1984, and we were all invited—all of us, that is, except Bill. Although both Rick and Bill were full brothers, Bill had always been closer to Pat than to our father. Warren thought that Pat would try to interrupt and spoil the wedding if she knew about it, so he didn't invite Bill for fear he would tell his mother when and where it was being held. Warren warned us not to mention the wedding to Bill.

My brothers and their wives were already at my father's house in Fenton when I arrived. I said polite hellos to everyone then excused myself to unpack. Although I had talked to my father, I had only been back to his house once since 1979, and I was nauseated as I climbed the stairs to the second floor. The guest room where I was to stay was across the hall from my father's room. It was the same room I'd occupied before. Quickly unpacking my suitcase, I found a hanger for the dress I planned to wear to the wedding and hung it in the closet. I stood in the hallway, staring into the room where my life had taken a horrible turn.

Neither my brothers nor their wives looked up when I walked into the room where they had gathered. Some things never change.

The phone rang. It was Bill, calling for a ride from the Detroit airport. Furious that someone had slipped, whether accidentally or on purpose, my father shouted, "How did he find out about the wedding? Who's responsible for this?" No one said a word.

The wedding was a formal affair, held at a Catholic church. My brother Rick was the best man and the rest of the brothers were ushers. All Ann's children were there, either as bridesmaids or, like me, as guests. At the reception, I introduced myself to the man seated across the table from me.

He looked at me oddly. "Then you must have a sister," he said.

"No, I'm the only girl in the family," I said, wondering where he had gotten that idea.

"That's strange, because I was told that Warren had a retarded daughter."

I bit my tongue and smiled, hiding the anger. "I'm Warren's *only* daughter, I'm not retarded, and I have the papers at home to prove it."

Later that evening I danced with my baby brother, Bill, who was an amazing six feet, seven inches tall. I could barely reach his shoulders for the slow dance, so I stood on his size thirteen shoes while he moved me around the floor and we talked.

I was ten years old when Bill was born. As with my other brothers, we never really had a chance to get to know each other when we were growing up. Like me, Bill was hyperactive. He also had a rare disorder called Marfan's syndrome. People with Marfan's usually have trouble with their blood vessels and their heart, and Bill had surgery when he was seven to repair a hole in his heart.

Another characteristic of the syndrome is a tall, thin stature with long arms out of proportion with the rest of the body. Bill's height should have made him a natural on the basketball court, but his heart condition prevented his participation in sports.

I had never spent much time with Bill, and when Pat left Ohio she took Bill and Rick with her. The three of them came to visit the year I graduated from high school, and I arranged to meet Bill for lunch at his hotel. We were standing next to each other in the lobby; he recognized me, but I didn't recognize him until he called my name.

"Are you Bill?" I asked. I gazed up at the six-foot giant standing beside me. "I can't believe it's you! The last time I saw you, I was looking down at you, now I have to look up." We greeted each other with a hug.

Bill was animated and talkative at lunch that day, complimenting the waitress on her hair and her earrings when she brought our drinks and continuing the flattery when she returned to take our order.

I kicked him under the table. "Stop making a nuisance of yourself."

"I'm not," he said. "I thought she deserved a compliment."

I groaned and looked out the window while Bill asked the waitress about several menu choices, what they were made of and what they tasted like. Finally he made his selection and the waitress left.

"Will you cut it out? You're embarrassing me."

"But Anne, people feel better when you give them compliments."

"And they get embarrassed when you overdo it," I finished.

Bill wasn't finished. When the waitress brought our meal, he praised her, telling her that she had served him well. I rolled my eyes and sighed in exasperation.

While we ate, Bill told me about his school life. Because of Marfan's, he was very thin, with arms so long he could touch his knees without bending over. Pat bought his clothes at a shop specifically for tall men, which made him look older and provided more opportunities for teasing. He had a lot of trouble making friends and the other children teased him unmercifully, calling him "Giant" and other, less flattering names.

Bill insisted on treating me to lunch and I could see that it was useless to refuse. As we were leaving the table he lifted the salt shaker and put a ten-dollar bill underneath.

"Whoa, Bill, that's way too much. Our lunch was barely five dollars," I said, grabbing his arm.

"Don't worry," he said with a smile. "I've got enough money and, besides, she deserves it. Good help is hard to find these days."

I just stared at him. As we walked away, I looked back at the waitress, who was excitedly showing the bill to another waitress. Laughing, she cupped her hand to whisper in the other waitress's ear. Both of them were looking right at Bill. Although I couldn't read her speech, I could imagine what she was saying. Walking up to Bill, who was in line to pay the bill, I said, "Good help may be hard to find, but that waitress is making fun of you."

When it was his turn to pay he asked to speak to the manager. "Sir, our waitress, Becky, did an excellent job serving us. I just wanted you to know." The manager thanked him and we left, much to my relief.

"Do you always do that?" I asked. "Because if you do, you'll drive everybody up the wall." I couldn't hear the echo of my other brothers' criticism of me in what I had just said.

The next time I talked to his mother, I told her what had happened. "I'm not surprised," Pat said. "Bill isn't used to people being nice to him, so when someone is, he gets a little carried away with the compliments."

Suddenly I realized that I had treated him exactly like I had been treated all my life. Instead of accepting him as he was, I had been embarrassed to be with him—my own brother—who was more like me than any of the rest. What an idiot I'd been to forget the pain I'd endured for being "not normal," and what a fool I'd been to inflict it on someone else.

In the years since that lunch with Bill, I hadn't spoken to him even once until he showed up at the wedding he had not even been invited to. When it was time to leave, I gave him a ride to the airport, and we talked all the way. Talking about school was very painful. He told me of a party he gave for classmates and people he worked with. No one came. Unbidden, the memory of my humiliating pool party in Ohio surfaced and I could almost hear the cruel comments of the girls. My heart broke for him.

Because he needed to be in a warmer climate, Bill was going to a technical school in Dallas, studying to be a computer technician and working part-time to earn his spending money.

Like me, Bill had constantly begged our father for money to go to college but Warren refused, using Bill's chronic illness as an excuse. When Pat had pushed the issue with her lawyer, a financial plan had been arranged. Things went well for a while, he said. He had even saved enough money to buy a used car.

Then he began to fall behind in his schoolwork and had to quit his job to catch up on his studies.

So much of his life had paralleled mine. We both had suffered from delayed diagnoses of our medical conditions, had been neglected by our father because we were imperfect, and had been ignored by our siblings. The other brothers were gifted, talented, and . . . well . . . perfect, in our father's eyes, while we were slow and dull, an embarrassment to him. When we reached the airport, I was sad we couldn't spend more time together.

Two years later, Bill's lung collapsed. He had to return to Virginia for tests, which showed more extensive damage than he had thought. In June, four days before he was scheduled for surgery to repair a deteriorating aortic valve, Bill called to ask me to come see him in the hospital.

My first reaction was that it was impossible, and I told him so. I was involved in a special project at work and was scheduled to go out of town to conduct some road tests. Yet for the next three days I was unable to concentrate. Bill and I had never been very close and I hadn't seen him since the wedding, but he was still my brother. He had called because he needed my support, and I had turned him down.

I may have been physically at work but my mind was miles away. I was under a car, trying to remove the transmission, but I couldn't find the tools I needed or even remember which drawer of my toolbox they were in. My thoughts kept returning to Bill. I could think of nothing but my brother lying on the operating table with his chest open and his heart in the surgeon's hands.

Finally, I left my workstation, walked to the telephone, and in minutes I had a reservation on the next flight to Baltimore.

Six hours later I was at Bill's hospital in Baltimore. Nobody had told the hospital that I was coming, and at first the nurse on duty wouldn't let me see my brother. I had to show her my driver's license, proving that we had the same last name, before she would take me to his room. He was in a ward, but I had no trouble telling which bed was his. The hospital didn't have a bed long enough to accommodate his body and his feet hung over the end.

I walked to the side of the bed and could tell that he saw me because he tried to reach for my hand. He was still heavily drugged from the surgery. My eyes filled with tears as I sat beside him, holding his hand.

I had let him down. I hadn't been there before the surgery when he needed me. The realization that, once again, I had treated him like the others had always treated me was like a slap. Fear gripped my heart—fear that this was the last time I would see my brother alive.

I sat beside him for a long time with my eyes closed, imagining that I was giving him a hug, despite all the tubes and wires and monitors keeping him alive. Finally the nurse asked me to leave. In Bill's weakened condition, too much excitement would be bad for his heart, she said.

"Please don't make me go," I begged. "There's so much I have to tell him. I have to tell him I'm sorry."

The nurse held firm, though, so I got up and moved toward the door—then stopped dead in my tracks. I stared at the woman walking toward me. It had not occurred to me that she would be there, but of course she would be; she was his mother.

Pat reached out to give me a hug but I couldn't return it. A river of memories spilled over its banks, and I feared I would drown. But wait, this couldn't be Pat—this woman was too nice. Was this the same Pat who took me away from my grandmother and sent me to Margie when I was six? Was this the same Pat who dragged me out of St. Mary's? The same Pat who beat me with a hairbrush, who left me in the basement, beaten and bloody?

I felt my chest constrict and my vision grew blurry. *No! I can't have a seizure now!* I thought, as the panic threatened to overtake me. I went to the bathroom and splashed cold water on my face then walked until I found a café. I needed a place to think, to compose myself before going back to the waiting room.

When I began to feel stronger, I returned to find Pat sitting outside Bill's room. As I sat down beside her, she took my hand. She told me of her struggles with her son's failing health and the financial burden of his schooling. She told of her conflicts with my father, his refusal to pay child support, and his constant moving to avoid his responsibility for their two sons. She was troubled, and lonely. It was clear that she loved Bill. But of course she would—he was her natural-born son, whereas I had just been a burden. I felt sympathy for her sons but not for her.

I stood up and walked to the window, wondering where the nearest hotel was. In the reflection I saw my father walk in, stride past Pat as though she weren't in the room, and come straight to me. I stiffened as he enveloped me in a hug. We sat down together; Warren continued to ignore Pat and talked to me as if nothing was wrong—as though nothing had happened six years before, as though he didn't have a son near death in the next room—making small talk about my flight and my job.

Pat finally grew tired of being ignored. Once they began talking, they both talked at once. I caught threads of the conversation when Pat raised her voice, and I was stunned. My brother—their son—had undergone heart surgery that morning, and they were arguing over money. Money! It was always about money! Even when I was on home visits from Stoutamyre, they had always argued about money.

My father had removed Bill's name from his insurance policy when he turned eighteen. Pat wanted to know how he expected her to pay for the cost of this surgery and hospitalization, even working two jobs. She begged Warren to help her pay for their son's medical expenses, but Warren refused.

"I've waited a long time to be free of child support payments and extra insurance, and I'm not going to start it over again!" he shouted.

Tired of trying to follow the conversation and even more tired of the arguing, I stood up and walked to the doorway of Bill's room, watching him sleep and remembering the last few times we had been together. We were more alike than I had known. Perhaps he had sensed it too. Had we grown up together we might have been friends.

To my surprise, Pat invited me to stay the night with her. I was even more surprised to find myself accepting her invitation, and we sat up for a while talking. I told her about my job with GM and that I had taken a job in a factory because my father wouldn't give me money to go to college. I told her about the wedding and my father's coworker who had heard about Warren's retarded daughter. I told her about the test I had taken at the University of Michigan and about the results. She politely tried to listen, but I could tell that her thoughts were with Bill, so I dropped the subject.

The following morning I flew back to Michigan, certain that I would never again see Bill alive. And I was right. He was able to go home for a short time, but six months later my father called to tell me that Bill had passed away.

I flew to Washington, D.C., and stayed with my oldest brother and his family until everyone else arrived, then we drove to Richmond for Bill's memorial service. Everything was fine until I went to sign the guest book at the funeral home.

As I stood there reading some of the other names, one name leaped out at me: Stoutamyre. One of the guests was a relative of Margie's. I stood frozen, my eyes raking the crowd. Who was this woman and why was she here?

Just then Pat walked up, arm in arm with a woman she introduced as Margie's cousin Nora. I felt the color drain from my face as I stood there, speechless. She seemed happy to see me and told me that I looked well and that Margie had loved me very much. But her smile disappeared when I mentioned that I was writing a book about my life and would send her a copy when I was finished. She was the first person I told about the growing manuscript I was working on, and it felt good to see the sudden flash of understanding in her eyes. She had at least *some* knowledge that my time at Margie's school hadn't been filled with teddy bears and lollipops.

During the service I sat with brothers on both sides of me. Suddenly I began to experience what I know now to be a type of flashback, similar to those caused by post-traumatic stress disorder. Chest pains made breathing difficult, and I felt dizzy and lightheaded. I was losing control, shaking and sobbing. My father turned to look at me, and I imagined him wondering why I was crying so hard for a brother I hardly knew. But it was more than grief for Bill.

After a few minutes I realized that meeting Margie's relative had triggered long-suppressed memories of Stoutamyre School. In all the years since leaving there I had not dealt with the trauma. I had refused to talk about it even with the doctors at Chelsea Hospital. I wanted to find Nora again and tell her how Margie, who supposedly loved me so much, had caused me such pain. I wanted to scream in her face, to describe the beatings, the room with no lights or windows. To tell her what it was like to eat someone else's vomit, or eat food off the floor, or spend the night tied to a chair. I wanted to tell her of the lifetime of emotional pain her cousin had sentenced me to.

And why was she here at all, reminding me of Margie and intruding on my last time with my brother?

I breathed slowly and deeply. I had to calm down and concentrate on Bill. I saw my father watching me. Then Pat caught my eye and mouthed, "Are you OK?" I just looked away. How could she even ask?

After the Mass, all my turmoil was still right at the surface. When my father came over and put his arm around me, I twisted away, furious that he would touch me. "Tell me that you love me, after all you've done to me all my life," I said through gritted teeth. "Tell me that you love me after what you did six years ago."

His wife saved him from answering. "What's going on?" she asked.

The fury unleashed by the sight of the name in the guest register roared through me.

"Go ahead, Father," I spat. "Go ahead and tell her what's wrong. Tell her what you did to me. Tell your sons that you loved Bill after you told his mother that you didn't want anything to do with him." Not waiting for an answer, I shouted, "Tell your wife I'm retarded!"

As the conversations around us ground to a halt, they both told me to stop creating a scene. I turned and walked into another room.

Pat walked in, reached into her purse, and handed me a small pill. "Here," she said. "It'll help you relax."

Ann had followed Pat into the room. She grabbed my arm but snarled at Pat. "Don't you be giving her any pills. Come on, Anne, you're going with me."

"Leave her alone. She's not going anywhere with you." Pat grabbed my other arm and I became the prize in a human tug-of-war.

Shaking myself free of them both, I walked outside into the sunlight and fresh air.

Fifteen months after Bill died, my grandmother passed away. While I was at St. Mary's, I felt as though she had abandoned me, and later when she moved in with us after Pat went back to Virginia, I felt overprotected by her. Later, when I told her some of what her son had done to me, and allowed his wife to do to me, she accused me of lying. The love and affection I had felt for her as a young child had been nearly destroyed.

My father, Ann, three of my brothers, and I flew from Detroit to Newark, New Jersey, for the funeral. Mark (now a surgeon at the Mayo Clinic) was coming later. Peter would be flying in from Oregon with his eighteen-month-old daughter. Warren rented a large van so the whole family could drive together to my grandmother's old home. Although my cousin had bought it from her when she moved in with us in Ohio, many of my grandmother's belongings were still there and I could almost feel her presence as I walked around the house.

After we checked into our hotel rooms and had dinner together, my brothers spent the rest of the evening drinking beer and exchanging memories of our grandmother. I stayed with them for a while then went for a walk and retired early.

The following day, after breakfast, we visited with relatives until it was time to go to the funeral home. At one point, Peter leaned over and whispered, "Grandma told me not too long ago that she was ready to go."

When the services were over we took turns going up to the casket. Peter and I walked up together, Peter holding his daughter. As we stood there I began to remember all the good times with my grandmother, of her love for me. How sad that we had grown apart. I wished I had spent more time with her, so that we could have rekindled the warm relationship that used to mean so much to both of us.

13

One Thanksgiving we were all at my father's house in Ann Arbor. We were sitting around the table in a "food coma" while one of my sisters-in-law went to the kitchen to bring in the pies. As soon as there was a lull in the conversation I spoke up, telling everyone that I had made plans for the summer: I was going to Virginia to visit Pat.

Pat was eager to have me visit because she was trying to start a new life with a clean slate. In the last several years, her youngest son had died and her marriage to my father had officially ended. Now she only had her father and Rick and she was very lonely. She was trying hard to be part of her stepchildren's lives again, and I guess she thought repairing her relationship with me was a good place to start.

"What? Are you nuts?" one brother asked. "Don't you remember what she did to you? She doesn't care anything about you. Can't you think of a better way to spend your time?" It was ironic that he thought I shouldn't go to Pat's house because of how she had treated me—all my brothers knew was that she had sent me away to school. They still didn't know about the abuse I had endured.

"I'm going to ask her to take me back to Stoutamyre," I said. "I want to get some pictures for my book." That didn't go over too well, either. Nobody had been pleased that I was actually writing a book about my experiences. My family told me that writing about everything would only cause more pain—of course, they meant cause *them* pain.

For what seemed like a long time, no one said anything, and then my father spoke up. "I think you're making a big mistake going down there. What good can possibly come of it?"

"Let her do what she wants," said Mark.

"I can't believe you'd want to face that woman again," said another brother. "Why do you want to live in the past anyway? You'll just stir up old memories. You should be looking to the future and getting on with your life." This was a common sentiment among my family when I mentioned anything to do with Stoutamyre.

How could I explain to them that I needed to see it all again? I needed answers. I needed to know why Margie had treated me the way she did.

Yet I let their fears change my plans and the summer came and went without a trip to Virginia. I had decided to wait a while longer.

In the summer of 1987 I decided I was ready. I wasn't working a lot of overtime and could afford to take a few days off work. It was time to go visit Pat and ask her to take me to get my files from Stoutamyre. At first she tried to talk me out of going, but when I told her I wouldn't visit her unless she agreed to take me, she gave in.

I flew from Detroit to Richmond and Pat met me at the airport, looking the same as always—petite and impeccably dressed. When she walked over to give me a hug I felt nothing. Even though I didn't want to, I tried to hug her back but my arms were frozen at my side. I didn't feel the kiss on my cheek. The only sense that seemed to be functioning was my sense of smell: I recognized the perfume she was wearing.

Pat made dinner that night and we talked a little about my childhood. She said she had believed I was retarded because it had been in my medical records. Only when I was older and better able to communicate did she realize that I actually might be intelligent. Later that evening we went through some of Bill's things. She wanted me to take something to remember him by, but after watching the greed with which my family had claimed both Bill's and my grandmother's belongings, I preferred to just have the memories rather than material things. Pat seemed to want to start some sort of friendship with me, and I let her believe that I wanted it too. But all I really wanted was the trip to Stoutamyre.

Tired and nervous, I went to bed early that night. I had already begun having flashbacks of the car trips that had taken me to that place.

We left early in the morning and Pat drove from memory. I would not have known how to get there even with a map, but she knew all the roads and every turn. I tried to talk about Stoutamyre, but she still wouldn't listen to the story of the beatings and abuse I suffered there. She was so defensive that I gave up and focused on my own thoughts.

The trip was like a video being played in reverse. Time was reeling backwards as we made the last turn into the long driveway around lunchtime. There was no sign giving a name to the place. I got out of the car and slowly looked around. The playground had turned into a field of tall weeds, and the swings were red with rust. As we walked up the sidewalk I saw that the gym was in need of paint, and the shrubs that had been so small when I was there had grown into huge bushes. Weeds had forced their way through the black asphalt driveway, and the fence that separated the playground from the pasture was peeling sheets of white paint.

"Are you sure you want to do this?" Pat asked. "There's still time to turn around. We can drive right back to Richmond, if you want." The closer we walked to the main house, the more she was having second thoughts. She had no idea who lived there now and was afraid we might be intruding. Even worse, she was beginning to be afraid of the questions I might ask.

"No, this is something I have to do—something I want to do. I've waited a long time and now come all this way." I knocked on the door and waited.

A woman who appeared to be in her nineties answered my knock. We identified ourselves and explained that I had lived there twenty years before and had known Margie Stoutamyre. The woman's eyes widened and she looked away as though gathering her thoughts. She said she was Stella, and that her sister Margie had died two years earlier, leaving everything to her. I tried to start a conversation with her but she clearly didn't want to talk about Margie. Any other topic was fine, but when the conversation returned to Margie, her voice became hesitant and tense.

The woman said that she had had nothing to do with Margie's management of the place and she didn't know where the records were.

"May I please look around?" I asked the woman. To Pat, I said, "I'd like to go alone."

"Make yourself at home," the old woman said. As I walked up the stairs to the second floor, the movie continued to play in reverse. The memories crashed over me in waves and I fought to stay above them.

The iron-frame bunk beds still stood in what had been the girls' sleeping quarters, metal springs hanging low from years of use. Some had mattresses, but most didn't. Mine did. As I touched the mattress, thoughts and faces poured into my brain like a storm. How I wished for a pencil and paper to write down what I was remembering and experiencing.

As I sat there, I could see the ghosts of the children moving woodenly, in the robotic way of people in institutions. I could see my secret friend, who had woken me and then been beaten for it. And across the hall was Number 12, who had always been small and an easy target for Margie's wrath. I saw the children who had disappeared.

In the corner was the tall-backed chair that Margie had tied us to. I looked more closely and could see the rub marks on the front legs, where children had strained to loosen the straps or shifted to a different position. I remembered the beating I had gotten for running away and the long nights spent in this chair. The chair looked tiny in the dusty, lifeless room.

In between the two rooms was Margie's bed—just the mattress with no sheet. Her desk was covered with dust, and cobwebs connected it to the chair. In the bathroom, rust stained the sink drains and I could smell wellwater. I stood looking at the toilet, remembering Margie with a stopwatch in her hand.

I went back downstairs. Pat and Margie's sister were talking, but I couldn't recall who Pat was; it was if my mind had turned back in time to my childhood here. I felt like I was on another planet. I could hardly focus on one memory because so many were crowding for my attention.

I interrupted the conversation and asked Margie's sister if she knew about the root cellar. She denied that it existed. I took her to the spot in the floor where the trap door was and asked if she knew that Margie had kept us down there for days, in the dark. Pat told me to stop making up stories.

Next I found the other room, the room with no windows or lights. In the center of the ceiling was a light fixture with a pull chain, but no bulb in it. I had never seen the room in the daylight before and didn't know the light fixture even existed. I went to the corner I had lain in and then to the corner that had been my bathroom during the days I was kept there. Through the layers of wax a large discolored spot was visible on the wooden floor. Then I noticed similar spots all around the perimeter of the room. Each child sentenced to the room had his or her own sleeping corner and bathroom corner. Years of urine and blood from beatings had permanently discolored the wood. Only in the very center of the room was the floor unstained.

When I showed Pat and Margie's sister the room, I said, "See! I told you about this room but you didn't believe me. Here it is, just like I said. This is the room where Margie left us for days with no food or water. We slept on the floor and went to the bathroom in the corner. I wasn't lying. I wasn't dreaming and I wasn't making it up." I watched as the old woman turned and left the room.

Pat was getting angry. I left the small room, grateful to be out of there again, and went to the dining room. The table and chairs were still there, as were the ghosts of the children.

I went outside and walked to the huge old apple tree and found the spot where I had broken my leg. My mind was racing. I had to take pictures! I would never have this opportunity again. But instead I went to the swings, untangled one, and just sat there for a while, swinging back and forth like a little girl.

Then I was ready to go. My camera had dangled from my wrist throughout this visit to my past, and I hadn't taken a single photo. My eyes filled with tears as we drove back down the long driveway. As we turned onto the road toward town, I noticed that the road hadn't changed—the same gravel on the side, the same white lines on black asphalt, very little traffic.

I remember little of the ride back to Richmond. My mind was grabbing at images and bits of the conversations with the old woman, trying to put it all in perspective.

When I returned to Michigan, I was a mess. I had convinced myself I could handle anything on my own, without the help of medication. I was wrong. My visit to Stoutamyre triggered seizures, which had been few and far between for some time. I agreed with my doctors that I needed to take medication again, but it was six months before the seizures were finally under control. It would be even longer before I managed to assemble all the puzzle pieces of my trip back to Stoutamyre.

14

The same work slowdown that allowed me the time to visit Pat and Stoutamyre had another effect. I had worked so much overtime for so long that a regular forty-hour week seemed unusually short, both in time and in salary—I had become dependent on the additional money. I still planned to continue my education but thought that I should work on developing coping and social skills first. I hadn't had much of a social life for a while and thought I would like to begin to interact again with others my age.

I didn't want to join the deaf club again—I wanted to be accepted as *me*, as Anne, not as a woman who was deaf. I wanted to socialize with hearing people and have them see me as one of them. Since I had never been a big fan of the bar scene, I needed other ways to meet people.

I decided to go to the unemployment office, where I applied for a job cleaning houses. I got a job in August 1987, working for a woman named Anna. I got along well with my coworkers, who were all women, and found it easy to relate to the different customers. Not only did I start earning extra money, but I was on my way to finding some friends.

Anna and I soon began grabbing a bite to eat after work and occasionally going to a movie. Anna was a woman without visible flaws—hers were all on the inside, but in my desperate desire for a friend I didn't see those faults for a long time. Her husband, Aristidis, was powerfully built and handsome with smooth dark skin, dark hair and moustache, and dark eyes. One evening over dinner Anna told me that she and her family were planning to move to Greece. My heart sank at the thought of losing the person that I had been working on building a friendship with. When she asked me to come visit them in Europe, I was thrilled.

That spring, Anna and I became close friends, spending time together on the weekends and visiting her relatives. She often saw me agree to something, giving the impression that I fully understood when, in fact, I hadn't heard correctly. When Anna saw how my communication problems led to difficulties with banks, insurance companies, and so on, she stepped in to help. When tax time rolled around, she helped me find someone who "wouldn't take advantage of me." I felt that I had finally found a good friend who understood and cared about me. I didn't realize I was being set up.

The heat often failed in my apartment, so Anna helped me find a house in her mother's neighborhood. She went with me to the bank to help with the paperwork and arranged for gas, electric, and telephone hookups. I bought the house "as is" just to be able to move quickly into a place with heat. During the move, Anna's mother brought over wonderful home-cooked Greek meals.

The purchase of the house coincided with the return of overtime. When my finances stabilized I no longer needed to work two jobs. But when I told Anna I was quitting, she appeared hurt, saying that she needed me and that she had taken on additional jobs because I was working for her. She reminded me how she had helped me arrange for the house and had cooked for me and helped with my finances. Not wanting to appear ungrateful, I agreed to continue working for her.

Another reason why I kept working for her was that I could tell the business was in trouble. Anna never told me much about it, but I knew that she didn't have much money. I decided the extra work would be worthwhile if it meant Anna could afford to stay in the U.S. rather than move to Greece.

By July I had earned three weeks of vacation leave and saved $2,000 for my trip to Greece. I was eager to join Anna and her family, who had left in June. Because some American goods were very valuable there, Anna asked me to bring several pairs of blue jeans (which would sell for about sixty dollars a pair) and a pair of water skis. In addition, her mother brought over a suitcase stuffed with clothes and jars of peanut butter for the children, and asked me to include it with my luggage.

Anna met me at the airport when I arrived. No sooner did we arrive at the house then she began selling the blue jeans and the clothes that her mother had told me were for the grandchildren. Anna told me that the money would go into an account in all our names. She sold the water skis to her cousin, promising to add that money to our joint account as well. She also took my spending money, saying she would exchange it for Greek currency and keep it in a safe place for me until I needed it.

During the next three weeks I took a lot of pictures, spent a lot of time by the water, and gained nearly twenty pounds eating the rich food. Even though Anna had me rent a car, we seldom went anywhere except to buy groceries. Ari took the car to the bars in the evening. I only knew a few phrases in Greek and was afraid to go sightseeing by myself.

One night the three of us began talking about going into business together. I had no knowledge of owning or running a business, and I knew that I would have to rely totally on their judgment. I didn't want to risk losing my independence or the benefits from GM, so we agreed that I would provide some capital for the business and continue to keep my job. Over the years, my only major purchase had been the mobile home. With all the overtime and nothing to spend it on, I had accumulated a rather substantial amount of money in savings and in IRAs. And it was a good deal, I thought; the new business would allow Anna and Ari to move back to the U.S.!

Before I knew it, my three weeks were up and it was time to go home. A few weeks after I got back, Anna called to say that she and the children were coming back earlier than they expected. They were planning to move in with her parents until Ari joined them, but I asked her to move in with me instead. They would have plenty of privacy since I worked so much, and I would feel like I had a family to come home to. They moved in and Anna agreed to pay me $200 a month for rent. I closed an IRA and gave Anna nearly $23,000 to start our new business.

Looking back on it all, I can easily see that I was being taken advantage of again. But Anna simply would say exactly what I needed to hear to keep me under control. Listening to her smooth talk, I believed her and forgot about all my past problems with people. Anytime I began to get suspicious, she told me we were family, and that not only would she never take advantage of me, but that she would protect me from anyone who tried to. And I believed her. I was blinded by my need for a mother figure and a friend in whom I could trust.

Our business venture was called the Express Cleaning Company, and Anna was our manager. Good help was hard to find Anna said, so I would need to work to help get the business off the ground. I cleaned houses for six hours every day before my shift at GM; I should have made about $200 a week, but I never saw it. When I asked about it, Anna told me not to worry, that we were all in business together, and that as soon as the business took off I would begin to see the profits and be able to live like a millionaire.

By April I was working double shifts at GM as well as working six to eight hours a day for our cleaning company. Anna expected me to contribute all the overtime money (sometimes more than $1,000 a week) to our account. The cleaning business had grown to such a degree that it needed a van, she said. The company had purchased a Mustang with a personal loan from me. Using the Mustang for a trade-in, I purchased a van using my GM employee discount.

Work at GM was not going well. I was the only female in a crew of thirteen men who verbally and physically harassed me. This had been going on for eight months or more, and I couldn't take it any longer. I was dizzy, had terrible headaches, and at times could barely crawl from the car to the house when I got home. I was on the verge of both a physical and a mental breakdown and more than once had thoughts of suicide. It didn't occur to me at the time that I was working myself to death.

A few days off work helped enormously and I began to feel better, but Anna, without my knowledge, called GM to say that I was seriously disabled and couldn't come to work at all. I don't know exactly what she said, but she made it sound a lot worse than it was because she was trying to get me a medical retirement. She apparently provided them with medical proof because from that point on, my disability insurance made the payments on the van while I worked full-time for her.

Anna began taking care of my paperwork and bank transactions while I was sick. When I told her that I felt well enough to look after my own affairs, she insisted that she should continue.

Ari moved back from Greece and into my house. In June, he and Anna suggested we purchase some real estate in Boca Raton, Florida, that we could use as a rental property. I agreed to let them use my money for the purchase in exchange for an interest in the actual property and in the rental income.

I stayed in Michigan and ran the cleaning business while Anna and Ari flew to Florida to close the deal on the house, promising to bring the contract back for me to sign. They returned, but had some excuse about why they didn't have the contract. When I asked about my share of the property, Anna became very angry and accused me of not trusting her.

"It's not a matter of trust, Anna," I said. "What if something were to happen to you? I'd have no proof that we were partners in buying the property. I'd have no legal way to collect the rent from the house or to sell the property and get my money back."

"Don't be silly, Anne," she laughed. "Nothing is going to happen to us. Your money is safe. It hurts that you think I'd take advantage of you after all we've been through together. After all, we're family, right? And family sticks together. Family trusts each other."

In my family, the others had always stuck together and I had been stuck on the outside. What did I know of family loyalty and trust? My trust had been betrayed more times than I could count. But I desperately wanted this to work, even though warning bells were beginning to ring.

I was under a great deal of stress and Anna convinced me that taking more of my medication (Tegretol for seizures and Prozac for depression) would help. Sometimes she would tell me that the doctor had called, telling me to double my dose. Or she would hand me a pill and a glass of water, saying that I had forgotten to take my medication. I became less able to think for myself. She had her lawyer draw up papers for me to sign, giving her my power of attorney. She took over all my banking, having me sign my disability checks for her to deposit, and deducting a generous salary for herself for helping me.

Under the influence of multiple doses of drugs, I convinced myself that Anna was looking after my best interests. I signed blank checks when she gave them to me. When she needed extra money for the business, she had me get cash advances on my credit cards. Before long I had maxed out several credit cards.

If life had been tough before, it was about to get worse. Even though I was on medical leave from GM, I worked from 7:30 a.m. to 4 p.m. cleaning houses, then from 11 p.m. to 3 a.m. with her husband, cleaning a racquetball club. Some days I fell asleep at the wheel of the car before leaving the driveway. Between the high doses of medication, overwork, and lack of sleep, I was again approaching burnout.

One of the doctors I was seeing suggested that I be evaluated for severe mental depression at Sinai Hospital's Hearing-Impaired Professional Services Clinic in Detroit. Anna, who insisted on going with me, dropped me off in front, and told me to wait while she found a parking place. She said not to talk to anyone until she got back.

A woman came out and lit a cigarette. "Hi, my name is Kathy Surowiec. I'm one of the therapists here. Do you have an appointment?"

"Hi, Kathy. I'm Anne," I said. "Yes, I have an appointment. I'm waiting for someone who's parking the car."

"Well, would you like to wait inside where it's cooler?" she asked.

"No, we agreed to meet outside so I'd better wait right here," I replied.

Kathy finished her cigarette, ground out the butt in the sand-filled receptacle and went back inside just before Anna rounded the corner. We walked in together and found the correct office. Kathy was standing behind the reception desk when we arrived.

"I'm so sorry we're late," Anna said, appearing frustrated. "Our car broke down and we had to wait for the repair truck."

Anna didn't realize that Kathy and I had already met. Kathy told me later that Anna's lie sent up red warning flags about her. She instinctively knew not to trust Anna, an ability I was just beginning to develop.

My appointment was with Dr. Keith Lepard, the head psychiatrist. An interpreter was there and so was Anna, who did a lot of talking. Anna had told me to focus on GM, so the doctors would sign off on my medical retirement.

Dr. Lepard determined that I should start seeing a therapist once a week as an outpatient. I was pleased when he assigned me to Kathy, but Anna was upset because she knew Kathy could see right through her. And she was right: during our sessions, Kathy kept bringing things to my attention regarding my relationship with Anna's family. However, even though I was getting a better idea of what my "friends" were doing, I often told Anna what I talked about in therapy. Naturally, she tried to talk me into changing therapists. She knew that the more Kathy learned about my home life, the more of a threat she became.

Kathy began encouraging me to ask Anna and Ari to move out, but whenever I mentioned it to Anna she got upset and threatened to hit me. Anna was pregnant with her fourth child, which was her argument for being allowed to stay. After all, what kind of friend would evict her pregnant housemate?

I was very unhappy. Since Anna had moved into my house she had taken over every aspect of my life—my money, my friends, my time, when I should work, when I should sleep. I had no freedom, but whenever I tried to talk to her about it she insisted that we were in this together. We had a common goal, she said: to earn as much money as we could, then move out of Michigan and start a better life in Florida. She kept saying that I was part of her family, and that Greek families stick together.

She really got upset when I told her I wanted to go back to work for GM when I got better.

One night, still deeply depressed even after taking a lot of Prozac, I went for a walk and ended up at the airport. I walked around for a while and must have looked like a zombie. I climbed the stairs to the second floor and walked to the balcony. Leaning over the railing, I watched the flow of travelers—businessmen with their briefcases, families with young children, senior citizens in wheelchairs being pushed by airline employees. I wondered how their lives could be so different from mine.

I began to review all the reasons I wasn't happy; the answer was always: Anna. How could I get out of this mess? I wanted to go back to work for GM. I didn't care about the harassment; I would put up with anything to have my job back. I wanted my life to be the way it was before Anna entered it. I felt so alone, isolated from my family and any friends I had had. Kathy was the one positive point in my life, but she couldn't be with me twenty-four hours a day like I wanted. It always came back to my wanting a mother/friend.

I continued to look over the railing. People moved around me, everyone with someplace to go. I heard rumbled noises but couldn't make out what was being said.

I thought of all my meetings with doctors and therapists over the years and began to think that everything would be easier if I just took my life. What was life, anyway, if you couldn't hear what was going on around you? I felt incomplete without my hearing. Anna often said, as my father had, that I could hear when I wanted to, but it wasn't true and their words hurt. If only I could hear what was going on, I would know what Anna was saying when she talked on the telephone to my banks, doctors, and insurance companies. I'd know what she was saying when she talked with her back turned so I couldn't read her speech.

I lifted one leg over the railing and looked down at the shiny floor. I thought about what a mess my body would make on that freshly polished surface, and that someone would have to polish it all over again. I thought about the news coverage my suicide would get—*then* I would get noticed. "Deaf Woman Leaps to Death at Metro Airport," the headlines would read. It made me happy to think of Anna reading about my death in the *Detroit Free Press.* Then she could have her wish—she would get all my money, my house, and my car. GM wouldn't have to worry about me anymore. And I wouldn't have to worry about trying to make friends. People might still make fun of my speech if I was dead, but, hey, I wouldn't be there to know about it.

I was halfway over the railing, struggling to get the other leg over. All I had to do was put the other leg over and let go of the railing. I looked around and saw that no one appeared to notice what I was doing. Then I got mad. No one would care if I killed myself. Then I had a horrible thought: What if I didn't die? What if I just became a vegetable and had to be in the hospital hooked up to machines? That would be even worse than now. Anna would still have my money, house, and car and could come to the hospital and laugh at me for being such a fool. I visualized people standing around my bed in the hospital, laughing and talking too fast for me to understand.

And then I would be left alone to die slowly.

I pulled my leg back to the safe side of the railing and stood with both feet on the floor. No, I didn't want to die that way. Taking a deep breath, I turned and found a phone to call Kathy.

Kathy arranged for me to be admitted to Sinai Hospital for a few days while the doctors had me try different types of antidepressants. During my stay I saw a therapist daily, and even though I tried to focus on GM as Anna told me, little by little information about my home life slipped out.

When it was time for me to be discharged, Kathy asked at her church if anyone would be willing to have me move in for a few weeks while I continued with outpatient therapy. She wanted to keep me away from Anna so I could break her hold over me. A woman named Mary Beth responded.

Anna didn't like the idea of my staying with someone else, and she and Ari took me out to dinner on my first night at Mary Beth's. During the meal they tried to persuade me to move back home, assuring me that I would be better off in familiar surroundings. When I went back to Mary Beth's I was so upset that I vomited up my meal. Yet I stuck it out, staying with Mary Beth for a month and building up my courage.

In November, shortly after I moved back into my house, Anna and Ari and I had a huge argument over my lack of trust, complete with accusations of how many different ways that *I* had taken advantage of *them*. I asked Anna and Ari to move out of my home that night, but they still wouldn't go. I felt like I was in prison. Later that night, I went into the kitchen and found one of Anna's favorite knives and slept with it under my pillow for a week.

More and more I felt used. I had to do whatever Anna said to do. I had to tell the doctors what Anna said to tell them. I couldn't make any calls from my house unless Anna knew who I was talking to and what it was about. Anna wouldn't let me eat any of the food in the house, saying it was all for her children. Then when I asked for money—*my* money—to buy food for myself, she told me there was not enough.

One day I went to my room and lifted the pillow. There was my friend—Anna's knife. I looked at my reflection in the blade and saw a poor, silly fool. I had no trouble slashing my arm—once, twice, three times. Ah, the pain! I wanted to feel more pain, so I did it again. I cleaned up the blood, wrapped a towel around my arm, and left the house.

I walked for miles, furious with myself both for not being able to speak my mind and for the way things had turned out. I ended up at the Livonia police department, miles away from home. I decided to come up with a story so they would put me in jail. Jail would be safe. Jail would be better than living with Anna. Anything, I thought, would be better than living with Anna—even Stoutamyre.

I thought that if the officers heard the word "kill," they would put me in jail. I certainly had enough blood on me to have killed someone. I went in the public bathroom at the station and cut my arm some more, then walked up to the desk, showed them my arm, and told them that I had killed my stepmother.

Everyone began talking at once and, as usual, I couldn't follow the conversation because they were talking too fast. The next thing I knew I was in a holding area and Kathy had been called. I was taken to the medical center in Westland for stitches and admitted to Sinai Hospital for ten more days, leaving Anna in complete control of my finances.

After I was discharged and went home I felt worse than ever. Every time Kathy's name came up, an argument followed. Anna knew now that I had told Kathy a lot of the events of the past year and she pushed me to change therapists.

Anna and Ari were planning to go to Florida again in December and wanted me to go with them. But I knew that my name would never be on the title to the property, so I didn't want to see the house that could have been mine. By this time I realized that even the money they had used to buy their half of the house had come from my bank account.

Kathy arranged for me to be admitted to the Lafayette Clinic. I was going to be able to get away from them after all!

15

The two days before going to the Lafayette Clinic were tense. Ari kept asking me why I wanted to go to the "cuckoo house" instead of going to Florida with them. I was on edge and felt like running away. Finally the day came to be admitted. Anna went with me, coaching me all the way, telling me to focus on GM. What she was really saying was, "Don't tell them about us."

I arrived at the clinic filled with anger, hate, and confusion. I didn't know what the word "assertive" meant and had certainly never applied it to any areas of my life. Children are taught to obey, and at Stoutamyre absolute obedience was enforced in the cruelest possible ways. Later Pat had tried to mold me into her idea of a female child, failing to realize that I had been programmed for five years to behave like a robot. At school I was a social outcast, and at work I was ridiculed and rejected. In personal relationships my lack of social skills and communication made it easy for my "friends" to take advantage of me.

All of these experiences explained why I had problems with money, friends, work, and relationships. I had always given everyone anything they wanted and then more. I had never put myself first in life; I always deferred to others, whether they were family members, coworkers, or friends. It was easier to let others have what they wanted than to be accused of being selfish for standing up for what I wanted. I had been used in every possible way, and my dignity was destroyed.

It was time to pick up the scattered pieces of my existence and try to reassemble them into a whole life again. I had come to the Lafayette Clinic at the right time.

During the first two weeks at the clinic I cared about nothing and no one. I had a nightmare and woke up screaming one night. One of the attendants found me in the bathroom banging my head against the wall. The next thing I knew I was strapped into a chair with a helmet on my head, which brought more flashbacks of being restrained at Stoutamyre. Suddenly the nurse became Margie in my mind and I screamed, "Let go of me! Please don't tie me up any more!" But I knew Margie was dead, that it was my mind playing tricks on me. Sobbing and vomiting, the next two hours were difficult and I had to force myself to calm down. When I was released from the chair, I vowed that I would never again lose control of my violent emotions. I never wanted to be tied up again.

My treatment plan was made up of many different programs, including individual therapy, group therapy, and participation in a group that focused on women's issues. Other activities dealt with social skills, occupational therapy, and recreation therapy. There was a drama group, an aerobics class, and even a math class. Once a week I met with a self-awareness group and learned to recognize my own identity and build self-esteem.

In the beginning I had a difficult time shaking Anna's influence, and felt guilty revealing the events of the past year to the therapists. Having Anna and Ari out of my life made it easier for me to open up about the situation at home. At my therapist's suggestion I called them and told them I wanted them to move out of my house. In spite of everything that had happened, I felt as though I were betraying Anna. My guilt weighed me down until eventually I told Anna what I had told the therapists. Then I felt pressure from both sides. As awful as things had been, I still couldn't quite let go of the relationship with Anna. I thought that if I let go of her friendship there would be nothing left of me. Also, I wasn't used to talking about my feelings and it made me uncomfortable. Eventually I began to trust the doctors more, at first simply because they were there and Anna was not, then because I could see that they truly had my best interests at heart.

As I began to feel better, I had my mail forwarded to the hospital and began taking care of my personal business. It didn't take long to realize that I was very low on money. When I asked Anna to give me some she refused, saying that she didn't have any. For a year, anytime they had needed money, I'd given it, but when I needed money she wouldn't help.

This time I didn't *ask* them to leave, I *told* them. And this time they did.

As I began to share the story of my life with the doctors, I also started to reconstruct the journal I had kept in high school, which Linda had destroyed. The doctors provided me with loose-leaf paper and a ballpoint pen, and I began by writing my earliest memories. The medications I was taking helped to keep me calm during the writing but I often had flashbacks at night. Now, instead of banging my head against the wall, I wrote. I wrote about Margie, Warren, Pat, St. Mary's, Ruth, Glenn, and Anna. I wrote about my mother—how angry I was that she had left me with no mother, that it was her fault that nobody taught me all the things that she was supposed to have taught me as a child. And as I filled the pages, I could see the book that I had used to threaten Nora Stoutamyre was actually becoming a real possibility.

All the different programs helped me to grow both mentally and emotionally. After a time I began to realize that I really did possess the strength to meet different situations in life. I learned the importance of taking care of myself first and learned to deal with anger and stress. I began to feel better about my life and myself. Then another storm rolled in.

My father and Ann came to see me. Apparently someone from GM had contacted him for information about me and told him where I was. Warren appeared sincere as he told me that he wanted to help me any way he could—that he wanted to be there for me. At first I felt as though I was living in a dream. Could this be true after all that had happened in the past? I was terribly confused and felt as though I were betraying myself by even listening to him. But I sat through the visiting hour making polite conversation and wishing the whole thing was over. After they left I felt as though I'd been in a tornado. I isolated the pain and locked it away again and then I felt all right.

Ten days later my father returned. By then, I had told the doctors about the rape. The hospital staff knew the anxiety my father's visit would cause me and they told me I could refuse to see him. Yet I decided to deal with the situation directly and went down to the lobby to see him. He was in a good mood, smiling and cracking jokes. We made small talk for a while, until—with a jolt—visions of the past flooded my mind and I couldn't think clearly. I told myself that I was strong enough to handle them, but my emotions were working against me. He told me he wanted to talk to the doctors, that he thought it would help. I told him that I didn't want him to but he wouldn't take no for an answer.

When I finally couldn't take it anymore I got up and walked back to my room, thinking that I should just walk to the window and jump out. I felt guilty for walking away without telling him exactly how I felt. I tried again to tell myself that it had all been a dream; that no father would hurt his own flesh and blood. No father would turn his back on his own child. But it was no dream. And this time I had walked out on him. Suddenly I felt better. I felt ready to go home.

Just before I was discharged from Lafayette, my social worker told me that my father had written a letter to a Michigan state senator, complaining that the doctors would not release any of my information to him. He wanted to know what was going on. He had no control over me and he didn't like it. The director of the clinic explained that I was an adult and that my records were private unless I gave permission to have them released. I found out later that my father wrote to all my brothers telling them that I had been admitted to a state mental institution. They each sent a card but none of them came to visit me.

I left the Lafayette Clinic in June, nearly eight months after I had arrived. I remember the last day, walking to my car with my suitcase in hand, turning to look back at the building. "Thank you, Lafayette Clinic, for helping me," I said quietly. I knew that even as I was leaving, I was taking a part of the clinic with me in my heart.

After my release from the clinic, I returned to a house that had been stripped nearly bare. Anna and Ari had left the furniture but had taken the dishes, pots and pans, tools, and even the cabinets on the walls. I went to garage sales to replace the kitchen supplies. Anna still had my power of attorney and had signed the title for the van over to herself. I changed the locks on the doors and traded in my car in case they had made extra keys to it.

In all, Anna and Ari had sweet-talked me out of more than $80,000. What a price to pay for friendship.

Later I wrote a letter to each of my brothers telling them that our father had raped me. I put each letter in an envelope, and addressed and stamped them. Then I put them in my safe deposit box, waiting for the right time. I told myself that the next time I got mad at my father I'd mail them. But I could never bring myself to do it; something inside me told me to let go of those feelings. Eventually I cleaned the box out and threw the letters away.

Life after the Lafayette Clinic didn't change but my approach to it certainly did. I had been given the tools to take charge of my life and to cease being a victim. It wasn't going to be easy and I knew it, but I had survived this long for a reason.

After I had been out of the clinic for a while I went to visit an acquaintance. She wanted to know why I didn't wear makeup or dress in a way to attract men.

"How do you ever expect to have a boyfriend? You could be attractive if you fixed yourself up," she said.

Her father-in-law was there, and he said he knew I could make someone a good wife. He even knew someone who could make me happy, he said.

I ignored them, hoping they would change the subject if they saw I wasn't interested. No such luck. For some reason it bothers some people to see me without a boyfriend. They kept on until my assertiveness training took over. I told them how it was with me.

"The old me did what anyone wanted me to do," I said. "I went out with whomever anyone thought I should go out with. I wore fancy clothes, tight skirts, high heels, low tops, and lots of makeup—all to attract men who thought they could get in my pants. I did what others thought was normal. But guess what? I wasn't happy. I was lonely, confused, and suicidal. I went to the Lafayette Clinic to get myself together and learn how to be my own boss. And it worked! I'm in control of my life. I can go to bars and parties if I want. But I don't choose to live that kind of life. This is the way I am."

Looking back, I realized that some of the worst problems had happened after Ruth and Glenn moved to Florida. Not only had I lost my mentors, but I also had stopped going to church. While at the clinic, I realized I had hit rock bottom. As I saw it, when I was discharged I had three choices: I could either go back to the life I was living before, I could kill myself, or I could start going back to church. Church was obviously the best choice!

I vowed that within a month of my discharge I would be regularly attending church—or I would kill myself. I even marked the day on the calendar. I had a suicide plan and took precautions to ensure that I would be successful. First I would close and lock the garage doors and windows. Then, before tying myself to the worktable (in case I changed my mind) I would start my car. I even marked on the floor where the car would be parked and had the ropes laid out on the table.

On the first Sunday after my discharge, I went to church. And the next. And the next. When the day I had marked on the calendar arrived I realized that I no longer needed the ropes. I threw them away, scrubbed the mark off the floor, and raised the windows to let in the warm, fresh summer air.

After I began attending church regularly, all aspects of my life began to improve. I took better care of myself and saw my therapist regularly. At last I had some control of my life. I believe now that I am living my life the way God wants me to live it and this is the path I will stay on.

Of course my life would have been easier if someone had sat me down and laid out the rules of life. But my life had taken a different path and there was no use continuing to say, "if only." *If only my mother hadn't died. If only Pat had been a decent person and had loved me. If only someone had discovered my deafness earlier. If only I'd been allowed to live with my grandparents. If only I could have stayed at St. Mary's.*

That kind of thinking was destructive and served no purpose. Even now in my mid-forties, it's still hard to realize that I don't have a mother. Every year I find myself shopping for Mother's Day cards before I remember I have nobody to give them to. But I've made a lot of progress and I'm learning how to take care of myself—to be my own "mom."

I've learned to focus on today, on protecting myself. I regained $13,000 from Anna and Ari in an out-of-court settlement to a lawsuit. But more importantly, I got back my passport, my power of attorney, the will in which I had left everything to "my best friend, Anna," and anything they had with my signature on it.

I began doing volunteer work in the community. Every Saturday I went to Angela Hall, a nursing home for retired Catholic nuns. I enjoyed helping out there, partially because they reminded me of the sisters at St. Mary's. Once, I even got some of the sisters to dance when the mother superior wasn't looking.

Education, in many forms, has been my passion for the past seven years. I began by taking classes in things I was interested in to get used to being back in school. I took classes in home improvement, money management, and vegetarian cooking, and I attended self-help workshops to learn how to better myself and improve my ability to relate to people. Then I began with the academics. I had always been good in math, but the English language and I had never gotten along. English isn't a logical language, and my analytical mind could never figure out why the rules applied in some cases and not others. I drove my English teachers crazy.

I then began attending Madonna University, a private Catholic university in Detroit, to work on a degree in business.

My original goal was to start a home-based business so I could control my work hours and have more time to devote to volunteer work. Unable to find the right business, I've started computer classes.

I've made a number of good friends, whom I trust, and they often ask if I ever hope for reconciliation with my family. While I truly believe that my father and brothers love me, each in his own way, I continue to live on the fringes of my family. I am more than physically separated from them; I am emotionally separated as well.

This was made clear to me at a family reunion several years ago. We had rented some cabins on a lake in northern Michigan. It was a beautiful weekend, and there were facilities for horseback riding, sailing, and fishing. One night we all went out to a restaurant in a nearby resort town. Tables were moved together to accommodate our large family. During the dinner, Rick said something and the rest of the table erupted in applause and cheers. He had brought his girlfriend with him and it occurred to me that they might be engaged, but when I looked at her hand, there was no ring. I assumed it must be something else.

I nudged one of my other brothers to ask what was going on. With a quick wave of his hand, he indicated that he would tell me later. The laughter and excitement continued. I got the attention of another brother across the table but he didn't want to interrupt the conversation he was wrapped up in. He, too, gave me a sign that he would tell me later. My father was sitting next to me but he was very involved in a discussion and I couldn't even get his attention. Ann motioned for me to wait because my father was busy.

I sat, looking around the table at the pockets of conversation, wondering why I had even bothered to come. I knew that if I got up to leave, no one would notice.

Twenty minutes later a small pocketknife was passed around the table. Engraved on it were the words, "Will you marry me?" After dinner someone explained that my brother and his girlfriend had climbed Mt. Rainier and at the top he had proposed by giving her the knife.

By the time the knife got to me, the excitement of the moment had already passed and I had no one to share it with. It was like getting the punch line of a joke after everyone else has stopped laughing. I went back to my cabin and shed tears of loneliness for the family I had never had.

During the following month I contacted each of my brothers to refresh their memory about the engagement announcement. I wanted their help to work out a strategy for avoiding this situation at future family gatherings. None of my brothers could understand why I was making such a fuss. One said that I was using my hearing impairment to get attention. Another said I used it as a crutch to get out of doing things I didn't want to do. Still another said that there was nothing wrong with my hearing and that I should put more emphasis on others rather than myself. My father had done a thorough job of convincing them that I faked a hearing loss to get attention. They all considered me self-pitying and selfish. Since then my involvement with my brothers has decreased.

If I'm meant to be in contact with my family, then it will happen. We were never allowed to have a normal relationship, and we have all gone our separate ways. This used to bother me more than it does now. My involvement in the church and my volunteer work help fulfill my desire for a family. I've also recognized that I need support from other people with a hearing loss.

As a person who is hard of hearing, I'm not always accepted in the hearing world. On the other hand, some deaf people don't accept me because I can speak. Nevertheless, I still participate in both the deaf and the hearing worlds. It's a lot easier to socialize and make friends within the deaf world because we share the same language. But when I go to the bank, grocery store, gas station, or work, I have to deal with hearing people. So I'm finding a place for myself in both these worlds.

I recently attended a silent retreat sponsored by the deaf club in Detroit. Beginning Friday evening, only sign language was allowed, and "voice cops" collected a dime for each spoken word. (I took ten dollars in dimes just in case.) All introductions were in sign and no one told if they were deaf, hard of hearing, or hearing. This was to avoid labeling. After all, is someone less deaf if she lost her hearing as the result of an automobile accident as an adult? In some ways that person may suffer even more discrimination than someone who was born deaf; no one will believe that she is deaf because her speech is so good.

Without planning it, I was the leader of a breakfast meeting on Saturday morning. We all shared our difficulties in dealing with hearing people and everyone had a story to tell. I encouraged them to consider writing a book or a newspaper article describing life as a person with a hearing loss. Even people with perfect hearing today could become deaf as a result of an accident, an illness, or simply the aging process. We learned a lot from each other, and some of the members encouraged me to work with their organization. It felt good to be able to offer help and advice and to be respected for my accomplishments.

On Sunday when we could start talking again, many were surprised to hear me speak. I still correspond with some of the people I met at the retreat, and I'm looking forward to going again.

This book has grown all my life—first as a journal, then as therapy, and finally with the hope that sharing it will help others. As my life started to improve I began to believe that reading about my experiences might help others. I want people to know that they can create their own destinies. I have learned from all the experiences in my life, both positive and negative, and have gained from them the strength not only to survive but also to overcome any obstacle that may come my way. I know I'm not perfect and that there will be other stumbling blocks, but I also know that there is nothing I can't handle with God's help.

EPILOGUE

Meeting Adair Renning in January 1998 was the beginning of the realization of a dream. I had always talked about writing a book, and it was finally going to happen.

In the process of helping me organize my manuscript into a book, Adair made a phone call to St. Mary's to get my exact admission and departure dates. The sister in charge told her of a reunion in July to celebrate the fiftieth anniversary of St. Mary's of Providence Center. The sisters were trying to contact as many former students as possible to invite them to the reunion. I don't know if they ever would have found me if not for that telephone call.

As soon as the invitation arrived, Adair made reservations for herself, me, and Kathy. (Over the years Kathy has heard every detail of my life and wanted to be a part of this reunion.) We would fly to Philadelphia on Saturday and drive the following morning to St. Mary's.

The early morning rain had thinned to drizzle when we checked out of the motel. As we left the four-lane highways for the Pennsylvania countryside, the roads narrowed until the trees formed a canopy above us. The actual drive took much longer than any of our instructions had said, but we didn't mind. The scenery was beautiful: farmhouses and fields alternating with dense woods as though we were traveling back in time.

Even without the signs marking the way I began to recognize the area. As we passed the black iron fence I knew we were close, and just around the corner was the spiked iron gate, just as I had remembered it. The gate was closed but a sign pointed the way to the parking lot.

The sun was shining and the air was warm as we walked toward the chapel. It was as though I had turned the clock back thirty-three years. Everything looked the same, even the air smelled the same as I remembered. The chapel was filled and there was little room even to stand. After a few minutes Adair and I tiptoed out, leaving Kathy inside. We signed the guest register and stepped into the sun. I couldn't wait any longer to see the old buildings.

The grounds were empty—everyone was inside the chapel—so we had the place almost to ourselves. As we walked, the memories poured over me. This place, my safe haven between two wars (the Stoutamyre War and the War with Pat) had not been my imagination. It was real and it was still standing, virtually unchanged. After all I had been through at Stoutamyre, St. Mary's had seemed like paradise. How appropriate that the sign above the entrance to the chapel read, "Our Paradise on Earth."

The main mansion, which had been our home, seemed untouched by time. We walked to the front entrance and up the stairs to the porch and to the double doors on the right. Everything was closed while all the residents and guests attended the mass, so we went back to the walkway and around to the rear of the property, past the chapel and the building that had been the gym. New buildings had been added to accommodate the senior citizens who lived there now, but all the older buildings that I remembered were still there.

In the back a huge white tent shaded the reception area where tables were covered with white tablecloths and fruits, salads, pastries, roast beef and rolls, and sub sandwiches. On the grass were large tubs filled with ice and soft drinks. Not wanting to miss Kathy leaving the chapel, we walked back up the path just in time to see the sisters walking out in a group. I had been told that Sister Martha (the first person in my life to suspect that I had a hearing problem) would be there. I spotted her right away. Of course, after the sisters passed us, I couldn't tell which one she was; they looked alike from the back. I grabbed Adair's arm and pulled her to where the sisters had stopped. Walking around the group, I found Sister Martha and lightly tapped her shoulder.

The tiny woman turned around. "Sister Martha?" I asked, although I knew even after thirty years.

Turning, she said, "Yes?"

"Are you Sister Martha?" I asked again. "I'm Anne. Do you remember me? You took care of me when I was learning to ride a bike and ran into the wall." I grabbed her hand and placed it on my head where the knot remained.

She remembered. Smiling and laughing, we hugged each other as the rest of the sisters watched. I stood holding both her hands in mine. These were the hands that had taken care of bumped heads and scraped knees, given us cold medicine and rubbed our chests with salve when we had coughs, and given us snacks every day. I cried and didn't want to let go. As we hugged again I noticed how tiny she was. The Sister Martha of my memory had been tall, and when she shook her finger at us, we knew she meant business. Those hands had showed me real love when I needed it most.

Sister Martha was in her seventies now and healthy except for deteriorating vision. She had stayed at the school for many years, and it pleased me to think of how many other young women must have benefited from her patience, wisdom, and love. I wanted to stay with Sister Martha but I knew we couldn't take all her time, so I asked permission to tour the mansion. We hugged once more and I promised to see her again before we left.

We walked in a side door that took us to the rear of the main entrance, just underneath one of the sets of winding stairs. Ahead of us were the carved, arched wooden doors that led into the activities room. It was difficult to contain my excitement because the inside of the building was all the same, exactly as I had remembered it. The furniture had changed and was now more suited to adults than children, but the structure was the same.

I found the curving stairs to the second floor where my room had been. We only had permission to tour the main floor, but after seeing the stairs I knew I had to go up. One of the sisters told us that Sister Bernadine was the mother superior, and we left to look for her and get permission to go upstairs.

We were also looking for Sister Mary. But during the time period when I was at the school, there were several nuns there with that name. No one we asked could agree which Sister Mary was "mine." Adair got as many phone numbers as she could to try to track her down for me, but we never did end up locating the woman who had taught me the meaning of love.

Back outside, we decided to take advantage of the buffet luncheon while we looked for Sister Bernadine. Someone pointed her out to us, and just as we finished eating, she walked by our table. We approached her with our request. I think she was about to say no, but a younger sister identified herself as Sister Collette and offered to take us upstairs.

My heart was racing as we walked back into the cool interior of the stone building. As Sister Collette started up the first set of stairs, I stopped her. We had never used those stairs as children. My room was up the other set of stairs.

"It's all right," she said. "We can get from one side to the other once we're upstairs."

At the top we turned left and walked through a large room that had been a classroom thirty years before. Walking out the other side of the large room we were at the top of the other set of stairs. I recognized it immediately and began walking down a short hallway in the direction of my old room. I retraced the footsteps of the child I had been.

The room was laid out exactly the way I remembered it, and I walked straight to my old bed. Overcome with emotion, I began to cry. "My bed! That was my bed." My mind began replaying events from my past. I saw myself sitting on Sister Mary's lap, my head close to her heart as she sang to me. I couldn't hear the words but I could feel the vibrations of her chest. Many nights she sang the poor, terrified child I had been to sleep.

Reluctantly pulling myself back to the present, I looked around the room. The wooden floor had been carpeted, but the shutters that folded back beside the long, thin windows were the same. This was my safe room, and I wanted to stay there with my memories. I wanted to hold on to them and relive them all. But it was time to go. I turned to look at my bed one last time, thinking of all the children that had come and gone since I left. It didn't matter. I could still see the image of Sister Mary holding me to her heart.

As we walked down the stairs, away from my room and my bed, I knew that even though Sister Mary was not at the reunion, the memories of her and my year at St. Mary's would always be there, both in the room and with me.

When I saw Sister Martha for the last time, she was waving good-bye and smiling the same smile I remembered as a child. The black hair showing from under the cloth covering her head was now a beautiful silver gray.

I knew that I couldn't take Sister Martha with me, that I had to leave her there at St. Mary's of Providence. But I took the memories with me. I left the property with a smile and a sigh of relief—St. Mary's *had* been real, and I could go back to visit whenever I wanted. I remembered the last time I had left: I had been filled with fear as Pat had taken me away. This time I was filled with joy. I looked back the same way I had as a child and this time I was ready—ready to leave and move on.